history at so

THE REFORMATION
in EUROPE

Andrew Johnston

Hodder & Stoughton
A MEMBER OF THE HODDER HEADLINE GROUP

Acknowledgements page iv

British Library Cataloguing in Publication Data

Johnston, Andrew
 The Reformation in Europe. - (History at source)
 1. Reformation - Europe 2. Protestantism - History 3. Church
 history - 16th century 4. Europe - History - 1517-1648
 I. Title
 940.2'3

ISBN 0 340 61116 2

First published 1996
Impression number   10 9 8 7 6 5 4 3 2 1
Year   1999 1998 1997 1996

Typeset by Sempringham publishing services, Bedford
Printed in Great Britain for Hodder and Stoughton Educational, a division
of Hodder Headline Plc, 338 Euston Road, London NW1 3BH by Redwood Books, Trowbridge

CONTENTS

Acknowledgements

Cover illustration courtesy of Mary Evans Picture Library.

The publishers would like to thank the following for permission to reproduce copyright illustrations in this volume:

AKG London p. 43a; British Museum p. 51b, Jean-Loup Charmet p. 44b; Mary Evans Picture Library 43b, 46a & b, 49b; University of Amsterdam Library p. 51a.

(a above; b below)

The publishers would also like to thank the following for their permission to reproduce material in this volume:

The Lutterworth Press for extracts from H. A. Oberman, *Forerunners of the Reformation;* Addison Wesley Longman for extracts from B.M.G. Reardon, *Religious Thought in the Reformation;* Andrew Johnston, *The Protestant Reformation in Europe;* R.J. Knecht, *French Renaissance Monarchy;* R.J. Knecht, *The French Wars of Religion;* M. Rady, *The Emperor Charles V;* Blackwell Publishers for extracts from A.E. McGrath, *Reformation Thought: An Introduction;* A.E. McGrath, *A Life of John Calvin;* SCM Press for extracts from *Library of Christian Classics;* Oxford University Press for extracts from E. Cameron, *The European Reformation;* B. Kidd for extracts from *Documents Illustrative of the Continental Reformation;* Macmlllan Press Ltd for extracts from R.W. Scribner, *The German Reformation;* Manchester University Press for extracts from H.A. Oberman, *Luther: Man between God and the Devil.*

Every effort has been made to trace and acknowledge ownership of copyright. The publishers will be glad to make suitable arrangements with any copyright holders whom it has not been possible to contact.

PREFACE

The Early Modern period has been a popular area of study for Sixth Form historians. Recent years have seen the introduction of source-based questions by examination boards. The Reformation and, in particular, Luther and Calvin, has featured large in such areas of syllabuses.

This book is intended for students, and hopefully teachers, who are interested in the Protestant Reformation and who would welcome a practical complement to existing textbooks and monographs. Several topics are covered by an introduction and a collection of mainly primary sources, together with questions of the type likely to be encountered in examinations, or other exercises involving the use of sources. Practical advice is proferred on the way to approach such questions and a specimen answer is included. Guidance is also offered on the approach to essay questions. Sample essay titles are given along with suggestions on relevant approaches; and again, a specimen answer is included. Finally, a brief analytical bibliography is intended to give guidance to teachers and students alike.

A note on this collection of sources

It is the intention of this collection to give ideas to teachers and realistic examples of sources and questions to students, either for use in schools and colleges or for self-study purposes. However, they are intended to be flexible. If it is found helpful, adapt the questions or mark allocations, or devise new questions; or use the sources as part of coursework or personal studies. You might even find it an interesting exercise to put together your own sources and appropriate questions.

APPROACHING SOURCE-BASED
QUESTIONS

Source-based questions have become an important part of History examinations at all levels in recent years. Students who have studied History at GCSE and Standard Grade will be used to handling various types of sources. The skills you have learned in dealing with evidence will continue to be applicable at a more advanced level, but there will also be more sophisticated skills to master and the sources themselves may be more demanding.

During your studies you will encounter both primary and secondary historical evidence. The distinction between the two is sometimes artificially exaggerated; all sources have their value and limitations, and it is possible to worry unnecessarily about a 'hierarchy of sources'. The important thing for the student is to feel confident in handling all sources. The majority of sources in this book are primary sources, since they are the raw material from which historians work; and they are mostly of a documentary nature, since that is the type most commonly found in examinations. However, there are also statistics and examples of visual evidence. The comments below will usually apply to all types of evidence.

When a student is faced with a piece of historical evidence, there are certain questions that he or she should always ask of that source; but in an examination the student will be asked specific questions set by an examiner, and, in the light of pressures - not least of which is time - it is important to approach these questions in an organised and coherent fashion. The following advice should be borne in mind when answering source-based questions. Some of the advice may appear obvious in the cold light of day, but, as examiners will testify, the obvious is often ignored in the heat of the examination room!

Answering documentary questions

1 Read the sources carefully before attempting to answer the questions, whether it is one source or a collection of them. This will give you an overview of the sources which will usually be connected and related to a particular theme. You will study the individual sources in detail when you answer specific questions.
2 Always look carefully at the attribution of the sources: the author and date of publication; the recipient, if any; the context in which the source was produced. All these will often give you an insight in addition to that provided by the content of the source itself.
3 Mark allocations are usually given at the end of each question or

sub-question. Ignore the marks at your peril! The number of marks will almost certainly give you some indication of the length of answer expected. Length of answer is not an indicator of quality and there is no such thing as a standard answer, but it is commonplace for candidates in examinations to write paragraph-length answers to questions carrying one or two marks. A question carrying such a low mark can usually be adequately answered in two or three sentences. You do not have the time to waste your purple prose in examinations! Similarly, a mark allocation of nine or ten marks indicates the expectation of a reasonably substantial answer.

4   Study the wording of the questions very carefully. Some questions will ask you to use only your own knowledge in the answer; some will ask you to use both your own knowledge and the source(s); some will insist that you confine your answer to knowledge gleamed from the source(s) alone. If you ignore the instructions, you will certainly deprive yourself of marks.

5   If there are several sources to be consulted, ensure that you make use of the ones to which you are directed - candidates have been known to ignore some or choose the wrong ones.

6   Certain types of question require a particular type of response:
    (a) Comparison and/or contrasting of sources: ensure that you do consider all the sources referred to in the question.
    (b) Testing the usefulness and limitations of sources: if you are asked to do both, ensure that you do consider both aspects. You may be required to evaluate a source in relation to other information provided, or in the context of your own background knowledge of the subject.
    (c) Testing reliability. This is not the same as considering the utility of a source, although students sometimes confuse the two concepts.
    (d) Responding to phrases such as 'comment upon', 'analyse' or 'assess'. Ensure that you do what is asked. Do not be afraid to quote extracts from a source in your answer, but avoid over-quotation or too much direct paraphrasing, since questions will usually, although not always, be testing more than comprehension. You should therefore use quotations merely to illustrate or amplify a particular point. Always consider the sources and do not just copy what is in front of you.
    (e) Synthesis: this is a high level skill which requires you to blend several pieces of evidence and draw general conclusions.

7   If at all possible, avoid spending too much time on the sources questions in examinations. Frequently candidates answer the sources questions thoroughly but do not allow themselves enough time to do justice to the rest of the examination paper, and essay answers sometimes suffer in consequence if they are attempted last.

8   If possible, read published examiners' reports which will give you further informtion on the most useful approaches to particular questions, and the pitfalls to avoid.

3

1 LUTHER AS A RELIGIOUS THINKER

Historians normally date the birth of the Reformation as 31 October 1517, the day on which Martin Luther allegedly nailed his Ninety Five Theses to the church door in Wittenberg. In these Ninety Five Theses, originally written in Latin, Luther initiated what he imagined would be a scholarly debate on the doctrine of indulgences. Since 1342 the Church had taught that the purchase of indulgences (the surplus merits of Christ and the Saints) was a means of avoiding an act of penance after confession of one's sins to a priest. Since 1476 it had been possible to purchase indulgences for the dead and thus reduce their time in purgatory (a place of purification from sin) to speed their passage to heaven. As a result, in the popular imagination it was believed that one could purchase forgiveness. Luther called all this into question. He was goaded into action by the activities of an indulgence seller named John Tetzel, a Dominican monk who was peddling his wares nearby. Fifty per cent of the profits from sales was to contribute to the rebuilding of St. Peter's basilica in Rome.

The Ninety Five Theses created a sensational impact. This is because without Luther's knowledge they were quickly translated into German and then printed. Consequently they were discussed by an entirely different and much wider audience than was originally intended. Conservative theologians were quick to smell a rat. Since the doctrine of indulgences was backed by the Pope, any challenge to it was heretical because papal authority was unquestionable. Thus the crisis quickly escalated from a series of specific theological questions to all-out conflict on the issue of authority in the Church. By 20 June 1520 this had lead to Luther's excommunication.

At around the same time that he wrote the Ninety Five Theses - we cannot say exactly when for certain - Luther underwent a profound conversion experience. He came to a radical and new understanding of how a man could be justified or made righteous before God. Luther's training as a theologian followed a tradition known as the 'modern way'. According to this school of thought, by doing his very best, man was able to contribute something towards his own salvation as God would have seen his efforts and because of His promise bestow His grace. When Luther became an Augustinian hermit in 1505 he did so because this was, as he saw it, the surest way of pleasing God. He followed the monastic rule to the letter but, rather than bring him hope, Luther found that this left him in a place of despair. He knew that he was a sinner and that his sinful nature prevented him from performing righteous acts. How then could he please God and receive His grace? Luther came to the conclusion that he must be damned.

In 1512 Luther became Professor of Biblical Studies at the University of Wittenberg. The detailed examination of the Bible necessary for this new post began to change his thinking. In his autobiographical account of his conversion written some thirty or so years after the event, Luther implies that it was a sudden dramatic realisation in a single moment of time. In fact, his thinking changed gradually from 1513 when he first became critical of the 'modern way' to 1518 when he had entirely broken with his former views.

Luther's new understanding, the doctrine of justification by faith alone, was to become the cornerstone of the Reformation. It was a view espoused by Zwingli, Bucer, Calvin, indeed all mainstream Protestant theologians. They believed that righteousness was not a standard which man had to attain in order to receive the grace of God but a gift which was received on the basis of faith in Christ. According to St. Paul's letter to the Romans (1:17) 'The righteous [or just] man shall live by faith'. The believer remained a sinner but in God's eyes he or she was clothed in the righteousness of Christ.

It is possible to find a link between the doctrine of justification by faith alone and Luther's criticism of indulgences. Yet Luther was not explicit in his views on justification in the Ninety-Five Theses. Was it because his views on the subject were still maturing and he was still making concessions in his own mind? There has also been a debate on the Ninety-Five Theses. Were they intended as a series of statements for academic debate or as the blueprint for a Reformation of the Church, based upon a new doctrinal principle?

A Luther's Description of his Life as a Monk
I was indeed a good monk and kept the rules of my order so strictly that I can say: if ever a monk got to heaven through monasticism, I should have been that man. All my brothers in the monastery who know me will testify to this. I would have become a martyr through fasting, prayer, reading and other good works had I remained a monk very much longer.

From Martin Luther's letters

B Luther's 'Tower' or Conversion Experience
I hated the expression 'righteousness of God,' for through the tradition and practice of all the doctors I had been taught to understand it philosophically, as the so-called 'formal' - or, to use another word, 'active' - righteousness through which God is just and punishes sinners and the unjust. But I could not love the righteous God, the God who punishes. I hated him ... I was very displeased with God, if

not in secret blasphemy, then certainly with mighty grumbling, and said: should it not be enough for miserable sinners eternally damned by original sin to be oppressed by all sorts of calamity through the law of the Ten Commandments? Must God add suffering to suffering even through the Gospel and also threaten us with His righteousness and His wrath through the Gospel too? ... I pondered incessantly, day and night, until I gave heed to the context of the words, namely: 'For [in the Gospel] is the righteousness of God revealed, as it is written: 'The just shall live by faith.''' Then I began to understand the righteousness of God as a righteousness by which a just man lives as by a gift of God, that means by faith. I realised that it was to be understood this way: the righteousness of God is revealed through the Gospel, namely the so-called 'passive' righteousness we receive, through which God justifies us by faith through grace and mercy ... Now I felt as if I had been born again: the gates had been opened and I had entered Paradise itself.

From Luther's autobiographical fragment, March 1545

C   Luther Teaches that the Justified Man Remains a Sinner
What then? Are we sinners? No, rather we are justified, but by grace. Righteousness is not situated in those qualitative forms, but in the mercy of God. In fact, if you take mercy away from the godly, they are sinners, and really have sin, but it is not imputed to them because they believe and live under the reign of mercy, and because sin is condemned and continually put to death in them ... Surely ... it is almost greater to accept as righteous him who is still infected by sin than him who is entirely pure.

From Martin Luther, *Against Latomus* (1521)

D   The Medieval View of Justification
The term 'justification' means literally, 'to make righteous' before or in the sight of God. This interpretation of it goes back to St. Augustine, who regarded salvation as the free work of God, while conceiving of the grace (that which is bestowed gratis) whereby this is achieved as an infusion of supernatural life into fallen human nature by divinely appointed means, although his emphasis was on the divine impor- tation rather than on the human attainment. Thus sinful man is justified by being transformed into the image of Christ, justification and sanctification ('to make holy') being to all intents one and the same process. This Augustinian doctrine became the accepted pattern of medieval teaching, which acquired a standardised form in the *Summa Theologica* of St. Thomas Aquinas, where justifying grace is described as 'something real and positive' within the soul, an infused supernatural quality by which alone the 'theological' virtues of faith, hope and love, as constitutive of the Christian life, can be produced.

Moreover, in the nominalist teaching especially, particular stress was laid on the co-operative response of the will.

From B.M.G. Reardon: *Religious Thought in the Reformation* (1981)

E Selections from the Ninety Five Theses

(1) When our Lord and Master, Jesus Christ, said 'Repent...' he meant that the whole life of believers should be one of penitence.

(2) The word cannot be understood as referring to the sacrament of penance, in other words of confession and satisfaction, as administered by priests.

(5) The Pope has neither the will nor the power to remit any penalties beyond those he has imposed either at his own discretion or by canon law.

(6) The Pope can remit no guilt, but only declare and confirm that it has been remitted by God; or, at most he can remit it in cases reserved to his discretion. To ignore such remission would of course leave the guilt untouched.

(21) Hence those preachers of Indulgences are wrong when they say that a man is absolved and saved from every penalty by the Pope's Indulgences.

(27) It is mere human talk to preach that the soul flies out [of purgatory] immediately the money clinks in the collection-box.

(36) Any Christian whatsoever who is truly repentant has, as his due, plenary remission from penalty and guilt, even without letters of Indulgence.

(81) This wanton preaching of pardons makes it difficult even for learned men to redeem respect due to the Pope from the slander or at least the shrewd questionings of the laity.

(82) For example: 'Why does not the Pope empty purgatory for the sake of most holy love and the supreme need of souls? This would be the most righteous of reasons, if he can redeem innumerable souls for sordid money with which to build a basilica, the most trivial of reasons.'

From Martin Luther: Ninety Five Theses (1517)

Questions

1 How, according to Source B, did Luther's understanding of righteousness change? **(5 marks)**

2 Compare and contrast Sources B, C and D. Account for the differences between Luther's view of justification and that of medieval theologians. **(6 marks)**

3 How reliable are autobiographical Sources such as A and B as accounts of Luther's life? **(6 marks)**

4 From your own knowledge explain why Source E caused such a stir in Germany. **(6 marks)**

5 'Luther sought a break with Rome in 1517'. From your own knowledge and the Sources comment on this view. **(12 marks)**

2 LUTHER THE REBEL, 1517-21

In publishing the Ninety Five Theses Luther provoked a heated religious debate, not merely in the University of Wittenberg as he had intended, but throughout all classes of German society. Luther found an audience ready to listen. Urban communities, peasants and scholars alike were attracted to his ideas in the early 1520s for a variety of reasons. Undoubtedly, in the first instance his ideas received more attention in scholarly circles as a result of contemporary attacks on scholasticism made by Christian humanists. Erasmus and others like him had, since the late fifteenth century, been poking fun at popular superstition and criticising scholastic theology. Quite wrongly, as it turned out, humanists embraced Luther as one of their own and this helped give the German reformer's ideas greater credibility.

Luther's critics did not all emerge at once. On first hearing of events in Wittenberg Pope Leo X is reputed to have dismissed the business as no more than a monkish quarrel. This is not so foolish a remark as it first appears or as some historians have suggested. Initial divisions were very much along 'party' lines. Augustinians backed Luther as one of their own whereas Dominicans, long-time opponents of the Augustinians, came to Tetzel's defence. When the Augustinians did nothing to set their own house in order and failed to discipline Luther at Heidelberg in 1518, a Dominican named Sylvester Prierias took up the cause. Prierias's intervention was significant because he shifted the grounds of debate, attacking Luther not for his criticism of indulgences, but by suggesting that Luther's questionings were a challenge to papal authority and therefore heretical.

Some important issues arose from the Luther affair, and his appearance before Cardinal Cajetan at the Diet of Augsburg in October 1518 and his debate with Johannes Eck in June 1519 were especially significant. How effectively did Cajetan develop Prierias's argument on papal authority in his efforts to establish Luther as a heretic? At Leipzig Eck sought to demonstrate an ideological link between Luther and the fifteenth-century Bohemian reformer Jan Hus, who was burnt at the stake for heresy at the Council of Constance in 1414. How important were Cajetan and Eck in securing Luther's excommunication and what should we make of the secular verdict against him at the Diet of Worms in April 1521? It seems surprising that the young emperor, a Habsburg elected only two years earlier despite vigorous attempts by Leo X to block his accession., should endorse the papal ban. Why was it that Charles's loyalties to the Mother Church triumphed over specific appeals to German nationalist sentiments made by Luther to Charles in his *Address to the Christian Nobility of the German Nation* (August 1520)? There has also been a debate about the extent to which Luther's views had become increasingly radical and therefore unacceptable to Charles and whether it was only the political protection of Duke Frederick, his territorial prince, which saved Luther and his cause.

A The Response to Luther, 1517-21

In four years the 'Luther-affair' grew from an academic and ecclesiastical feud between two religious orders to set Germany (and much of Europe) by the ears. Luther had not sought such notoriety; nor was it due to his ideas and writings alone. Coincidences, born out of the context, helped to obscure the real issues of the affair, and exaggerate its importance. These same factors gave Luther supporters who would only fully understand his message rather later.

Luther's case did not immediately awaken widespread interest. To take but one example, in early 1518 von Hutten (a poet and author of fashionable dialogues) regarded the debate as a row between theologians, a class of people he detested. However, in the course of 1518-21 he and his type identified more and more with Luther's anti-scholastic and anti-papal (as opposed to theological) positions. Hutten suspected that Luther's opponent at Augsburg in 1518, Cardinal 'Cajetan', came to the Reichstag to preach crusade only to swindle money out of Germany. In his dialogues, entitled Fever the First, Vadiscus, or the Roman Triad, The Onlookers, and Fever the Second, published between spring 1519 and 1520 (a German translation appeared in time for Luther's appearance at Worms), Hutten popularised anti-papal polemic and sided more and more openly with Luther. He and Crotus saw Luther attacked by their own old enemies and warmed to him. Hutten and von Sickingen joined forces in mid-1520 and associated with other humanists such as Eobanus Hessus, Martin Butzer or Bucer (1491-1551), Johannes Hussgen or Husschin ('Oecolampadius', 1482-1531), and Reuchlin's great-nephew Philipp Schwarzerd ('Melanchthon', 1497-1560) who were later in one form or another to become leading protestant figures. Before the major implications of Luther's highly distinctive message had been fully absorbed, his broader and more familiar protests and proposals had won him a pre-existent party of enthusiasts who thought (wrongly) that his cause was the same one for which they had already been fighting. In due course the older humanists turned against Luther; the younger ones, on the other hand, were mostly converted to views which, in spite of the independence of mind and diverse characters of the formidable minds involved, were in their essence and implications remarkably close to Luther's own.

From E. Cameron: *The European Reformation* (1991)

B   Martin Bucer on Luther at Heidelberg
In giving answers his pleasantness was remarkable, in listening his patience was beyond compare; in his refutation you would have recognised the shrewdness of Paul, not Scotus, and with his replies so concise, so acute and drawn from the store of divine scriptures he easily led them all to admire him. The next day I had a private and friendly conversation with the man, remote from observation, and a meal long prepared and desired, not for its food, but its teachings. Whatever questions I asked, he explained very lucidly. All his views concur with Erasmus, except that he seems to excel in this one respect, namely that what Erasmus only implies, Luther teaches openly and freely. O if only I had the time to write more to you about this. He has brought it about that those small-minded writers of Wittenberg have been scorned to a man, while Greek writings - Jerome, Augustine and Paul - are publicly taught.

From a letter by Martin Bucer, 1518

C   Luther at Augsburg
They are all very cordial to me for the sake of the illustrious Elector. But although the very reverend cardinal legate himself promises to treat me with all clemency, yet my friends will not allow me to rely on his word alone, so prudent and careful are they. For they know that he is inwardly enraged at me, no matter what he may outwardly pretend, and I myself clearly learned this elsewhere.

But today, at any rate, I shall approach him and seek to see him and to have my first interview, though whether it will so turn out I do not know ... I know not whether the most reverend legate fears me or whether he is preparing some treachery.

Yesterday he sent to me the ambassador of Montferrat, to sound me on my position before the interview with himself. All think that the man came to me suborned and instructed by the legate, for he pleased with me long, advancing arguments for sanity (as he called it), saying that I should simply agree with the legate, return to the Church, recant what I had said ill ...

Then he went on to make some insane propositions, as, for example, he openly confessed that it was right to preach likes, if they were profitable and filled the chest. He denied that the power of the Pope should be treated in debate, but that it should be so exalted that the Pope might by his sole authority abrogate everything, including articles of faith, and especially that point we were now disputing on.

From a letter from Luther to George Spalatin, secretary to Frederick the

Wise, 10 October 1518

D The Leipzig Debate

Luther followed Karlstadt to sustain the thesis that it was only by recent decretals that the Roman Church was proved to be superior to other Churches, against which stood the authority of scripture and the Nicene Council. Eck left no stone unturned to overthrow this opinion; he summoned all the forces at his command, spending eight days on it and doing his best especially to make his opponent invidious by dragging in home Hussite articles. Luther at once understood the snare, and raged as though inspired by some spirit at being thus insidiously betrayed on a side issue. With great indignation he rejected some of the dogmas imputed to him, while embracing some of them as Christian, relying everywhere either on well weighed testimonies of scripture, or on the decrees of ancient councils. In short, his main effort was to remove far from himself the suspicion of favouring the Bohemian schism. Eck also bent his whole energy on impressing the audience with this opinion of Luther, no matter how much the latter rejected it. In like manner they debated on other things, the state of souls in purgatory, fear as the root of penitence, and Indulgences, consuming nearly twenty days in all.

From a letter written by Peter Mosellanus, an admirer of Luther, 7 December 1519

E The Views for which Luther is Condemned

25 The Roman Pontiff, the successor of Peter is not the Vicar of Christ over all the churches in the whole world, appointed as such by Christ himself in blessed Peter.

26 The word of Christ to Peter: 'Whatsoever thou loosest on earth' etc. (Matthew xvi) applies only to Peter's own binding (and loosing).

27 It is certain that it is not in the power of Church or Pope to fix articles of faith, or even laws of conduct or of good works.

28 If the Pope, supported by a large part of the Church, expresses this or that opinion - and a correct one at that: even so, it is neither sin nor heresy to disagree, especially if the matter is not one necessary to salvation, until a universal Council has approved the one view and condemned the other.

From the papal bull *Exsurge Domine*, 15 June 1520

F Charles V's Response to Luther

It is certain that a single monk must err if his opinion is contrary to that of all Christendom. According to his [Luther's] opinion the whole of Christendom has been in error for a thousand years, and is continuing still more so in that error in the present. To settle this matter I have resolved to stake upon this course my dominions and my possessions, my body and my blood, my life and soul. It would be a disgrace for me and for you, the noble and renowned German nation, appointed by peculiar privilege and singular pre-eminence to be the defenders and protectors of the Catholic Faith, as well as a perpetual stain upon ourselves and our posterity, if in this our day and generation, not only heresy but even the suspicion of heresy or the diminution of our Christian religion were due to our negligence.

After the impudent reply which Luther gave yesterday in the presence of us all, I now declare that I regret having delayed so long the proceedings against the aforementioned Luther and his false doctrine. I have now resolved never again, under any circumstances, to hear him. He is to be escorted home immediately ... with due regard for the stipulations of his safe conduct. He is not to preach or seduce the people with his evil doctrine and not to incite them to rebellion.

From the judgement at Worms, 19 April 1521

Questions

1 According to sources C and E which aspects of Luther's teaching were most objectionable to his religious opponents? **(5 marks)**

2 How do sources A and B help explain Luther's popularity and success in the period 1517-21? **(8 marks)**

3 From source D and your own knowledge explain why Luther might be said to have lost the debate but emerged triumphant from Leipzig? **(6 marks)**

4 Compare sources B and D. Account for the contrasting views Eck and Bucer had of Luther. **(6 marks)**

5 What light do these sources shed on the causes and consequences of papal and imperial hostility to Luther, 1517-21? **(10 marks)**

3 LUTHER AS A BIBLICAL THEOLOGIAN

Luther became a practical reformer but he was, first and foremost, a Christian theologian. In the months between the proclamation of the papal bull *Exsurge Domine* (June 1520) and the imperial ban (April 1521) the Wittenberg professor wrote perhaps his three greatest works. Put together, the *Address to the Christian Nobility of the German Nation* (August 1520), *The Babylonish Captivity of the Church* (September 1520) and *The Freedom of the Christian Man* (November 1520) completed the birth of a new theology. They also more or less guaranteed Luther's condemnation at the Diet Worms and thus had a decisive effect in shaping the politics of the Empire for the rest of the reign of Charles V.

The first of the treaties, the *Address to the Christian Nobility* was both political and theological in its purpose. Luther was well aware that if he and his ideas were to survive the onslaught of Roman opposition, he needed political allies. Hence, he sought to mobilise support by writing a pamphlet aimed at the ruling classes in German society - Charles V, the princes, nobles and city magistrates. In doing so, he was well aware of the forces of nationalism and the deep unpopularity of Rome in German society (antipapalism). Luther tapped into these feelings when he drew on existing arguments such as conciliarism (the belief that a General Council of the Church carried greater authority than the papacy) and formed new arguments. In particular, he discredited the notion that the clergy (priests) enjoyed superior status over the laity (ordinary Christians). Not only were priests corrupt, he argued, but they had no role to play as mediators in man's salavation. The doctrine of justification by faith alone meant that salavation was a private matter between God and the individual. This formed the basis for the doctrine of the priesthood of all believers.

The most extreme of all Luther's writings in this period was unquestionably his *The Babylonish Captivity of the Church*. At the heart of late medieval faith, devotion and practice lay the seven sacraments - baptism, holy communion, penance, confirmation, marriage, holy orders (the ceremony whereby someone is made a priest) and extreme unction, the administration of holy oil to the sick and dying. The Church, in dispensing these sacraments, administered grace or blessing to the Christian faithful. Luther destroyed this system. He disregarded four of the sacraments outright - confirmation, marriage, holy orders and extreme unction - on the grounds that they could not be sacraments since they were not bestowed specifically by Christ to the Church.

Penance was drastically reduced in importance and baptism left relatively unscathed. The really serious attack came on holy communion, also known as the Eucharist or the mass. Luther retained holy communion as a sacrament, but changed its meaning. Luther insisted that communion be administered in two kinds. Why was the mass rejected as a sacrifice or a recrucifixion of Christ? Why, despite these radical breaches with Catholic dogma, did Luther continue to assert his belief in the real presence, that is that the bread and wine of communion physically became the body and blood of Christ as the priest blessed them?

In the third of his great 1520 treatises of 1520 - *The Freedom of the Christian Man* - Luther developed and extended his ideas on faith. Since a man was justified or made righteous before God solely on the basis of faith in Christ rather than by works, it followed logically, Luther argued, that Christians did not *have to* comply with canon (that is, Church) law. However, this doctrine of Christian freedom presented new difficulties. Luther had to find ways to overcome any suggestion that he was advocating immorality or anarchy.

A Luther on Scripture and its Interpretation

In the first place, when pressed by the temporal power, they have made decrees and declared that the temporal power had no jurisdiction over them, but that, on the contrary, the spiritual power is above the temporal. In the second place, when the attempt is made to reprove them with the Scriptures, they raise the objection that only the pope may interpret the Scriptures. In the third place, if threatened with a council, their story is that no one may summon a council except the pope ...

Their claim that only the pope may interpret scripture is an outrageous fancied fable ... The Romanists must admit that there are among us good Christians who have the true faith, spirit, understanding, word, and mind of Christ. Why, then, should we reject the word and understanding of good Christians and follow the pope, who has neither faith nor the Spirit?

From Martin Luther: *Address to the Christian Nobility of the German Nation* (1520)

B Luther's Early Views on the Eucharist

1. The holy sacrament of the altar, or of the holy and true body of Christ, also has three parts which it is necessary for us to know. The first is the sacrament, or sign. The second is the significance of this sacrament. The third is the faith required with each of the first two. These three parts must be found in every sacrament. The sacrament must be external and visible, having some material form or appearance. The significance must be internal and spiritual, within the spirit of the person. Faith must make both of them together operative

and useful.

2. The sacrament, or external sign, consists in the form or appearance of bread and wine, just as baptism has water as its sign; only the bread and wine must be used in eating and drinking, just as the water of baptism is used by immersion or pouring. For the sacrament, or sign, must be received, or at least desired, if it is to work a blessing. Of course at present both kinds are not given to the people daily, as in former times. But this is not necessary since the priesthood partakes of it daily in sight of the people. It is enough that the people desire it daily and at present receive one kind, as the Christian Church ordains and provides.

3. For my part, however, I would consider it a good thing if the church should again decree in a general council that all persons be given both kinds, like the priests. Not because one kind is insufficient, since indeed the desire of faith is alone sufficient, as St. Augustine says, 'Why do you prepare stomach and teeth? Only believe, and you have already partaken of the sacrament.'

From Martin Luther: *The Blessed Sacrament of the Holy and True Body of Christ, and the Brotherhoods* (1519)

C His Views Develop

In all his promises, moreover, in addition to the word, God has usually given a sign, for the greater assurance and strengthening of our faith. Thus he gave Noah the sign of the rainbow (Gen. 9:12-17). To Abraham he gave circumcision as a sign (Gen. 17:11). To Gideon he gave the rain on the ground and on the fleece (Judg.6:36-40). So we constantly find in the Scriptures many of these signs, given along with the promises. For in this way also worldly testaments are made; not only are the words written down, but seals and the marks of notaries are affixed, so that it may always be binding and authentic.

This is what Christ has done in this testament. He has affixed to the words a powerful and most precious seal and sign: his own true flesh and blood under the bread and wine. For we poor men, living as we do in our five senses, must always have along with the words at least one outward sign to which we may cling and around which we may gather - in such a way, however, that this sign may be a sacrament, that is, that it may be external and yet contain and signify something spiritual; in order that through the external we may be drawn into the spiritual, comprehending the external with the eyes of the body and the spiritual or inward with the eyes of the heart.

From Martin Luther: *A Treatise on the New Testament, that is, the Mass* (1520)

D Luther Rejects the Mass as a Sacrifice

In the first part I have overthrown the devil's ungodly un-Christian priesthood and also proved that the mass may not be called a sacrifice. I have stopped up the mouths of the opposition so that they can bring up nothing in the way of counter-argument but their own dreams, customs, human wickedness and violence, all of which, as everyone knows, are worthless in divine matters and in establishing the faith.

In addition I have consoled those whose consciences are weak and have instructed them so that they may know and recognise that there is no sacrifice in the New Testament other than the sacrifice of the cross (Heb. 10:10) and the sacrifice of praise (Heb. 13:15) which are mentioned in the Scriptures; so that no one any longer has cause to doubt that the mass is not a sacrifice. Now, after this bickering, I wish in the second part to demonstrate the same thing through peaceful teaching and without any bickering and to build neatly on the foundations which I have laid, treating of the mass, not with our own words, as the devil's priests do with respect to their own mass, but with the divine words with which Christ himself instituted it.

From Martin Luther: *The Misuse of the Mass* (1521)

E   Luther Reduces the Number of Sacraments from Seven to Three
To begin with, I must deny that there are seven sacraments, and for the present maintain that there are but three: baptism, penance, and the bread. All three have been subjected to a miserable captivity by the Roman curia [papal government], and the church has been robbed of all her liberty. Yet, if I were to speak according to the usage of the Scriptures, I should have only one single sacrament (i.e. Christ) but with three sacramental signs, of which I shall treat more fully at the proper time.

From Martin Luther: *The Babylonish Captivity of the Church* (1520)

F   Luther on Christian Freedom
To make the way smoother for the unlearned - for only them do I serve - I shall set down the following two propositions concerning the freedom and the bondage of the spirit:

A Christian is a perfectly free lord of all, subject to none.
A Christian is a perfectly dutiful servant of all, subject to all.

These two theses seem to contradict each other. If, however, they should be found to fit together they would serve our purpose beautifully. Both are Paul's own statements, who says in 1 Cor. 9 (:19), "For though I am free from all men, I have made myself a slave to all," and in Rom. 13 (:8), "Owe no one anything, except to love one another." Love by its very nature is ready to serve and be subject to him who is loved. So Christ, although he was Lord of all, was "born of woman, born under the law" (Gal. 4:4), and therefore was at the same time a free man and a servant, "in the form of God" and "of a servant" (Phil. 2:6-7).

From Martin Luther: *The Freedom of the Christian Man* (1520)

Questions

1 Look at Source E. From your own knowledge explain why Luther reduced the number of sacraments from seven to three.   **(5 marks)**

2 Compare and contrast Sources B, C and D. How does the tone and emphasis of B and C differ from D?   **(8 marks)**

3 Using source A explain how Luther's understanding of the Source and nature of spiritual authority differed from that of his opponents.
                                                                   (6 marks)

4 Using source F and your own knowledge explain why Christian freedom was such an attractive doctrine.   **(6 marks)**

5 To what extent do Sources A-F support the view that Luther was a religious revolutionary?   **(10 marks)**

4 THE PRINCELY REFORMATION IN GERMANY

In writing the *Address to the Christian Nobility* (1520) Luther had sought, and failed to obtain, the support of the young and newly elected Emperor Charles V by appealing to the potent forces of German nationalism. Yet Luther did gain the political backing of some of the German princes early in his career. Indeed, when Charles V promulgated the Edict of Worms in April 1521 two of the elector-princes, Ludwig of the Palatinate and Frederick of Saxony had already somewhat conveniently left Worms and thus were unable to sign it.

In the following years Luther's support amongst the German princes grew. Albert of Hohenzollern, Philip of Hesse, the Margrave of Brandenburg-Ansbach, the Count of Mansfield, the Duke of Schleswig and the Duke of Brunswick were all converted to Lutheranism in the 1520s. The cause of the Reformation was assisted considerably in these years by Charles V's absence from Germany. Charles had left the Holy Roman Empire for Spain in 1522 in the wake of the *Comuneros* revolt in Castile. He remained there until 1529 and this seven year absence was crucial to the advance of the Reformation. Charles appointed his younger brother Ferdinand to act as his regent but was reluctant to grant him the necessary independence of action to crush the Lutheran challenge.

When Charles returned from Spain in 1529 he moved swiftly, calling the second Diet of Speyer which reinforced the Edict of Worms. This was to lead two years later to the formation of a defensive alliance of Protestant princes and cities known as the Schmalkaldic League. For the next fifteen years two rival armed camps faced each other in the Empire, but it was not until 1546 that Charles was in a position to declare war. He won a convincing victory the following year at the Battle of Mühlberg but failed to capitalise on this. Thus in 1555 he was forced by the terms of the religious peace of Augsburg to grant legal recognition to Lutheranism in those territories where the princes had converted to the new religion.

There is an interesting debate about the extent to which Lutheranism was hampered by the ambitions of its princely supporters. Were German princes inclined to lend Luther their support because they saw in the Wittenberg theologian a like-minded ally, suspicious of Roman justice and imperial authority? How important were the attractions of greater judicial freedom and the financial rewards of control of the Church; and how attractive to princes was the political prestige of being 'highest bishop' in their territories? It may be that the mixture of financial, judicial and political motives means that the princes were not as committed to Lutheranism *per se* as might first appear.

Some historians regard Lutheranism, by the end of the 1520s, perhaps even earlier, as having become a new orthodoxy, imposed from above. The laity were no longer encouraged to read the scriptures for themselves and come to their own conclusions, but, instead, these were given in the Word of God in bite-sized prepackaged chunks via the catechisms. How important was this in the elimination of false teachings such as the spiritual interpretation of the Eucharist which was so much more accessible than Luther's complex theory of consubstantiation? It can be argued that in this rapid transition from orthodoxy to heresy to new orthodoxy, the Reformation had come full circle.

A Luther Appeals to the German Princes for Support

To His Most Illustrious, Most Mighty, and Imperial Majesty, and to the Christian Nobility of the German Nation, from Doctor Martin Luther.

Grace and power from God, Most Illustrious Majesty and most gracious and dear lords.

It is not from sheer impertinence or rashness that I, one poor man, have taken it upon myself to address your worships. All the estates of Christendom, particularly in Germany, are now oppressed by distress and affliction, and this has stirred not only me but everybody else to cry out time and time again and to pray for help. It has even compelled me now at this time to cry aloud that God may inspire someone with his Spirit to lend a helping hand to this distressed and wretched nation. Often the councils have made some pretence at reformation, but their attempts have been cleverly frustrated by the guile of certain men, and things have gone from bad to worse. With God's help I intend to expose the wiles and wickedness of these men, so that they are shown up for what they are and may never again be so obstructive and destructive. God has given us a young man of noble birth as head of state, and in him has awakened great hopes of good in many hearts. Presented with such an opportunity we ought to apply ourselves and use this time of grace profitably.

From Martin Luther: *Address to the Christian Nobility of the German Nation* (1520)

B The Lutheran Church Service

Three serious abuses have crept into the service. First, God's Word has been silenced, and only reading and singing remain in the churches. This is the worst abuse. Second, when God's Word had been silenced such a host of un-Christian fables and lies, in legends, hymns, and sermons were introduced that it is horrible to see. Third, such divine service was performed as a work whereby God's grace and salvation might be won. As a result, faith disappeared and everyone pressed to enter the priesthood, convents, and monasteries, and to build churches and endow them.

Now in order to correct these abuses, know first of all that a Christian congregation should never gather together without the preaching of God's Word and prayer, no matter how briefly, as Psalm 102 says, 'When the kings and the people assemble to serve the Lord, they shall declare the name and the praise of God.' And Paul in 1 Corinthians 14 (:26-31) says that when they come together, there should be prophesying, teaching, and admonition. Therefore, when God's Word is not preached, one had better neither sing nor read, or even come together.

This was the custom among Christians at the time of the apostles and should also be the custom now. We should assemble daily at four or five in the morning and have [God's Word] read, either by pupils or priests, or whoever it may be, in the same manner as the lesson is still read at Matins; this should be done by one or two, or by one individual or choir after responding to the other, as may seem most suitable. ...

The lesson should be taken from the Old Testament; one of the books should be selected and one or two chapters, or half a chapter, be read, until the book is finished. After that another book should be selected, and so on, until the entire Bible has been read through; and where one does not understand it, pass on, and give glory to God. Thus Christian people will by daily training become proficient, skilful, and well versed in the Bible. For this is how genuine Christians were made in former times - both virgins and martyrs - and could also be made today. ...

In like manner, come together at five or six in the evening. At this time one should really read again the Old Testament, book by book, namely the Prophets, even as Moses and the historical books are taken up in the morning. But since the New Testament is also a book, I read the Old Testament in the morning and the New Testament in the evening, or vice versa, and have reading, interpreting, praising, singing, and praying just as in the morning, also for an hour. For all that matters is that the Word of God be given free reign to uplift and quicken souls so that they do not become weary.

The daily masses should be completely discontinued; for the Word is important and not the mass. But if any should desire the sacrament during the week, let mass be held as inclination and time dictate; for in this matter one cannot make hard and fast rules.

Let the chants in the Sunday masses and Vespers be retained; they are quite good and are taken from Scripture. However, one may lessen or increase their number. But to select the chants and Psalms for the daily morning and evening service shall be the duty of the pastor and preacher.

From Martin Luther: *Concerning the Order of Public Worship* (1523)

C A Lutheran Hymn

Dear Christians, let us now rejoice,
And dance in joyous measure,
That of good cheer and with one voice,
We wing in love and pleasure.
Of what to us our God hath shown,
And the sweet wonder he hath done;
Full early hath he wrought it.

Forlorn and lost in death I lay,
A captive to the devil,
My sin lay heavy, night and day,
For I was born in evil.
I fell but deeper for my strife
There was no good in all my life,
For sin had all possessed me.

My good works they were worthless quite,
A mock was all my merit;
My will hated God's judging light,
To all good dead and buried.
E'en to despair me anguish more,
That nought but death lay me before;
To hell I fast was sinking.

Then God was sorry on his throne
To see such torment rend me;
His tender mercy he thought on,
His good help he would send me.
He turned to me his father-heart;
Ah! then was his no easy part,
For of his best it cost him.

To his dear Son he said: 'Go down;
'Tis time to take compassion.
Go down, my heart's exalted crown,
Be the poor man's salvation.
Lift him from out sin's scorn and scath.
Strangle for him that cruel Death,
That he with thee live ever.'

The Son he heard obediently,
And by a maiden mother,
Pure, tender - down he came to me,

For he would be my brother.
Secret he more his strength enorm,
He went about in my poor form,
For he would catch the devil.

He said to me: 'Hold thou by me,
Thy matters I will settle;
I give myself all up for thee,
And I will fight thy battle.
For I am thine, and thou are mine,
And my place also shall be thine;
The enemy shall not part us.

'He will as water shed my blood,
My life he from me reave will;
All this I suffer for thy good -
To that with firm faith cleave well.
My life from death the day shall win,
My innocence shall bear thy sin,
So art thou blest forever.

'To heaven unto my Father high,
From this life I am going;
But there thy Master still am I,
My spirit on thee bestowing.
Whose comfort shall thy trouble quell,
Who thee shall teach to know me well,
And in the truth shall guide thee.

'What I have done, and what I've said,
Shall be thy doing, teaching.
So that God's kingdom may be spread -
All to his glory reaching.
Beware what men would bid thee do,
For that corrupts the treasure true;
With this last word I leave thee.'

From Martin Luther: *Concerning the Order of Public Worship* (1523)

D The Reform of a Bishopric

1. Hitherto ye have held seven sacraments, but not rightly. Henceforward faith must be before all things the foundation of your salvation, and he must have no more sacraments than Christ ordained, namely, Holy Communion and Holy Baptisms.

2. Henceforward no ban shall hold good which burdens the conscience without ground in God's Word, and is of force only by human institution.

3. Henceforward no confession shall be made to the priest, whereby a

23

man is bound to make known all his sins.

4. Henceforward there shall be no pilgrimages nor wanderings to holy places, since they aid no man's salvation.

5. Henceforward no processions shall be held, for they have no ground in God's Word.

6. Henceforward no ringing nor singing nor Masses nor Vigils for the dead are to be held: for they are of no use, and of no avail.

7. Henceforward no water, salt, ashes, palms, tapers, greenery, and the like are to be hallowed: for it is all nonsense and no good.

8. There are to be no obsequies and celebrations for the dead, and no prayers for them. For they are in God's hand and judgement.

9. There are to be no more Orders, neither monks nor nuns; but only such Orders as war against unbelievers and then, like the Teutonic Order.

10. Bishops shall continue and remain; not anointing-bishops or ordaining-bishops, but such as preach and teach and expound the pure word of God and preside over the Church.

11. Henceforward there are to be no superstitious distinctions made of days and seasons, with all sorts of Feast Days, Fridays, Saturdays, Ember Days, Fast Days, and so on; but every day alike shall be the Lord's Day, for eating flesh or fish as every man likes or finds necessary, or according as the good God may bestow it.

12. Easter, Whitsuntide, and Christmas, together with Sundays, are to be kept in Christian fashion, as is conformable to God's Word and order. Other such Holy Days as are not grounded in God's Word and keep men from their daily work and calling are sheer nonsense and fables, and conduct to bade example.

13. Hymns and prayers in church are to be in German, so that every man may understand. Salve regina is not to be sung, for it conduces to God's dishonour. Holy Baptism is to be administered in German, without chrism and oil.

14. Tithes are not to be given to priests who do not serve their office, but those who minister at the altar are to be paid from the altar.

15. In no church shall the Consecrated Bread be reserved nor taken for God's Body except at the Communion, according to Christ's institution, nor carried about.

16. Pictures in houses and churches are not be prayed to, nor to have any candles lit before them.

17. Allowing and forbidding of marriage on account of sponsorship is mere nonsense, and not grounded in God's Word.

18. Brotherhoods and guilds are to direct and lay out their endowments, not on the Mass, but on the maintenance of the poor and other pious uses.

19. The daily Mass is an abomination to God: so henceforward it is not to be observed in any church or anywhere.

20. When a man desires to go to Holy Communion, he must cause the priest, his confessor, to inform him out of God's Word, and must also inform himself, how he should receive and take the bread and wine according to Christ's institution in both kinds.

21. If any one thinks that he can make satisfaction for his sins himself or can save himself apart from the merits of Christ, let him be damned.

22. All priests and monks and nuns are at liberty to leave their orders and marry.

From the programme of reforms of the Bishop of Pomerania (1525)

E The Inspection of the Parishes of Saxony

Now that the gospel through the unspeakable grace and mercy of God has again come to us or in fact has appeared for the first time, and we have come to see how grievously the Christian church has been confused, scattered, and torn, we would like to have seen the true episcopal office and practice of visitation re-established because of the pressing need. However, since none of us felt a call or definite command to do this, and St. Peter has not countenanced the creation of anything in the church unless we have the conviction that it is willed of God, no one has dared to undertake it. Preferring to follow what is certain and to be guided by love's office (which is a common obligation of Christians), we have respectfully appealed to the illustrious and noble prince and lord, John, Duke of Saxony, First Marshall and Elector of the Roman Empire, Landgrave of Thuringia, Margrave of Meissen, our most gracious lord and prince, constituted of God as our certain temporal sovereign, that out of Christian love (since he is not obligated to do so as a temporal sovereign) and by God's will for the benefit of the gospel and the welfare of the wretched Christians in his territory, His Electoral grace might call and ordain to this office several competent persons. To this His Electoral grace through the goodness of God has graciously consented, and he has commissioned and commanded for this purpose these four persons, namely, the gracious and honorable Herr Hans of Planitz, Knight, etc., the worthy and learned Jerome Schurff, Doctor of Laws, etc., the honorable and constant Asmus of Haubitz, etc., and the worthy Philip Melanchthon, Master etc. May God grant that it may be and become a happy example which all other German princes may fruitfully imitate, and which Christ on the last day will richly reward. Amen.

From Martin Luther: *Instructions for the Visitors of Pastors in Electoral Saxony* (1528)

F Luther's Response to the Inspection of the Parishes of Saxony

Martin Luther to all faithful, pious pastors, and preachers:

Grace, mercy, and peace in Jesus Christ our Lord.

In setting forth this Catechism or Christian doctrine in such a simple, concise, and easy form, I have been compelled and driven by the wretched and lamentable state of affairs which I discovered lately when I acted as inspector. Merciful God, what misery I have seen, the common people knowing nothing at all of Christian doctrine, especially in the villages! and unfortunately many pastors are well nigh unskilled and incapable of teaching; and though all are called Christians and partake of the Holy Sacrament, they know neither the Lord's Prayer, nor the Creed, nor the Ten Commandments, but live like the poor cattle and senseless swine, though, now that the Gospel is come, they have learnt well enough how they may abuse their liberty.

O ye bishops, how will ye ever answer for it to Christ that ye have so shamefully neglected the people, and have not attended for an instant to your office? May all evil be averted from you! You forbid the taking of the Sacrament in one kind, and insist on your human laws, but never inquire whether they know the Lord's Prayer, the Belief, the Ten Commandments, or any of the words of God. Oh, woe upon you for evermore!

From the preface to *The Short Catechism* (1529)

Questions

1 In source A on what grounds does Luther appeal to Charles V and the German princes for support? **(4 marks)**

2 To what extent were Luther's aspirations in source A fulfilled in the 1520s and '30s? **(8 marks)**

3 In what respects do Sources B and C reflect an attempt to make Luther's theology accessible to the German public? **(7 marks)**

4 In what ways do Sources B and C differ in their purpose from Source D? **(5 marks)**

5 To what extent does Source F represent a betrayal of Luther's original ideals? **(5 marks)**

6 How much can 'official' documents such as Sources D, E and F tell us about the nature of religious belief in Germany in the 1520s? **(6 marks)**

5 THE URBAN REFORMATION IN GERMANY

Historians have long recognised the peculiarly urban qualities of the Reformation. There were some 65 imperial cities in Germany in the sixteenth century, that is, cities which were self-governing under the direct rule of the Emperor. More than 50 of these cities came to recognise Protestantism in some shape or form. Yet it was not merely in these proud and independent cities where the Reformation made its strongest impact. In the territories ruled by princes it was the towns rather than the countryside where the new religion first made its mark.

Political motives undoubtedly played a part in attracting city councils to the Reformation. By elevating the status of the laity and reducing that of the clergy, doctrines such as the priesthood of all believers were potentially appealing, since they enabled the lay magistrates to deal with the priests as equals. But there are other reasons for the urban appeal of Lutheranism. How important was preaching in Lutheranism's popular appeal? Viewed in a medieval context, the Reformation might be seen as a revival of popular preaching in the tradition of the fifteenth-century Florentine Girolamo Savonarola or the Franciscan and Dominican Orders founded in the thirteenth century. Such preaching had largely been an urban phenomenon and for good reason. Although the majority of the population of Europe lived in the countryside, the concentration of large numbers in the towns guaranteed an audience for preachers.

As well as preaching the message of the Reformation through the exposition of Scripture, Luther and his followers were also prolific writers. It has been calculated that there were perhaps as many as 10,000 different evangelical pamphlets published in Germany in the sixteenth century. It is therefore hardly surprising that cities such as Augsburg, Nuremberg, Stransbourg and Basel, all important printing centres, were also cities which were strongly impacted by the Reformation in the 1520s. Such cities enjoyed a far higher literacy rate than the rest of the Empire, so evangelical books had a wide and ready readership. Luther was prone to overstatement but was he exaggerating when he described printing as 'God's highest and extremest act of grace whereby the business of the Gospel is driven forward'?

A Support for Luther at Worms, 1521

April 25. I cannot tell you how much favour he [Luther] enjoys here, and which is of such a nature that, on the Emperor's departure and the dissolution of the Diet, I suspect it will produce some bad effect, most especially against the prelates of Germany. In truth, had this man been prudent, had he restricted himself to his first propositions, and not entangled himself in manifest errors about the faith, he would have been, I do not say favoured, but adored by the whole of Germany. I was told so at Augsburg by the Duke of Bavaria and many others, and I see the same by experience.

April 26. Luther is a man who will not relinquish his opinion, either through argument, fear, or entreaty ... He has many powerful partisans who encourage him, and against whom no one dares to [proceed] ... His books are sold publicly in Worms, although the Pope and the Emperor, who is on the spot, have prohibited them.

From the dispatches of Gaspar Contarini, the Venetian ambassador, 1521

B Popular Response to Luther
In the room we found one man, all by himself at a table with a book propped in front of him. He greeted us kindly and beckoned us to sit at his table. But our shoes were so muddy that we sat modestly at a bench by the door. Then he drank our health, which we could not refuse, and so reassured by his friendliness we sat down at the table to which he had bidden us, and returned his toast.

We took him for a knight, as he sat there, with a red hood, plain doublet and hose, a sword at his side, his right hand on its hilt, the other on his book. We said we had letters of introduction to some teachers in Wittenberg and asked 'Sir, can you tell us whether Dr Martin Luther is in Wittenberg just now, or else where he may be?' He replied 'I know for certain that he is not in Wittenberg at this moment'. And he strongly advised us when at Wittenberg to study Greek and Hebrew which were above all needful for the study of holy scripture. We said 'We have made this journey to see this man, for we have heard that he would overthrow priestcraft and the Mass, which he says is an unscriptural form of worship, while we have been destined by our parents from youth, to be priests'. And we marvelled at this knight who knew all about the teachers at Wittenberg, and how useful it was to know Greek and Hebrew; he also let slip an occasional Latin word so that we thought this must be a very uncommon knight.

This conversation having broken the ice my companion took the book from the man's hand - and found it to be the Psalms in Hebrew. My comrade cried, 'I'd have my little finger cut off if I might only learn this language'. To which the stranger replied 'You can soon master it, if you stick to it, as I am doing. I do a little bit each day.'

He asked us what they thought of this Luther in Switzerland (where we came from). 'Sir, there are many different opinions. Some cannot extol him too highly but others revile him as an unconscionable heretic, especially the clergy'. He said, 'That I understand - those parsons!' He paid for our dinner, and at it complained how the German princes and nobles assembled in Diet at Nuremberg on account of God's Word were only concerned with tournaments, sleigh rides … and whoring. 'But there's your Christian princes for you!'

Later the landlord told us the man was Martin Luther, and this really thrilled us, to have been the guest of such a man.

From a meeting between two students and Luther in disguise on his way back to Wittenberg in 1520.

C The Entry of the Papal Legate Campeggio into Nuremberg, 16 March 1524

We arrived at Nuremberg on the Wednesday in Passion Week. In these parts the sincere faith of Christ is utterly cancelled; no respect is paid either to the Virgin Mary or the saints. On the contrary, it is said that those who employ their aid sin mortally. They deride the Papal rites and call the relics of the saints bones of those who have been hanged. In Lent they eat meat openly, saying they do not consider it prohibited. Confession is neglected, as they say it should be made to God, and that auricular confession is a buffoonery. They generally communicate under both forms. They make a laughing-stock of the Pope and cardinals and other ambassadorial ecclesiastics, by means of paintings and other caricatures. In short, they consider Martin their illuminator, and that until now they have been in darkness, and the indulgences are held by them like bread sold in the market-place. In proof of all this, the Legate, to avoid scorn did not enter Nuremberg as Legate, neither did he give the blessing and absolution, but came in like a mere horseman, though he was accompanied by a most noble escort of all the Princes and part of the nobility, who (with the exception of the Duke of Saxony and Palatine) are sincere Christians. Some of the noblemen and the mass of merchants are all tainted, nay, obstinate and unconvertible, so that at present neither the Legate's authority nor the will of the Princes … can stem so strong a current.

Martin is not at Nuremberg, nor will he make his appearance there; but, unless the Almighty stretch forth his arm, it will doubtless come to pass that as the Princes and part of the nobility remain staunch Catholics, whilst the people persist in their errors, they will some day cut each other to pieces. The Legate will remain at Nuremberg until October, perhaps to hold another Diet in Germany but in this matter Diets profit little because the free towns are really not subject to any one, so that they cannot be curbed, and they are the abettors of Lutheranism, especially Nuremberg and Augsburg, the asylums of all converts. In the other towns belonging to the Princes less open confession is made but in short all are Lutherans, publicly or secretly.

From a letter by Friar Paolo Ziani, 29 March 1524

D The Mass Circulation of Luther's ideas

Canon: What does it mean to pray in spirit and in truth? Teach me so that I may pray in this way and then I shall need to say my matins no longer, nor say any other service.

Shoemaker: Read the little book written by Martin Luther entitled *The Freedom of the Christian Man* which he dedicated to Pope Leo X and there you will find it briefly explained.

Canon: I would rather that Luther along with all his books were burnt. I have never in all my life read any of them and nor will I, despite your advice.

Shoemaker: What! Why do you oppose them?

Canon: Because he does not worship the saints.

Shoemaker: Christ says 'You shall worship the Lord your God, and Him only shall your serve'.

Canon: Yes, but we must have intercessors before God.

Shoemaker: John says 'If any man sins we have a mediator before God, Jesus Christ the righteous, and He is also the peacemaker for our sins'.

From Hans Sachs: *A Dispute between a Shoemaker and a Canon* (1524)

E The Popularity of Luther's Message in the Imperial Cities
The imperial registers drawn up at the Diet of Worms in 1521 list a total of 85 cities under the title of 'Free and Imperial Cities'. At that time some 65 of these cities could be considered directly subject to the empire. The great majority of them, more than 50, in some way officially recognised the Reformation during the sixteenth century. Over half of the cities became and remained Protestant. Others permitted a Protestant congregation to exist alongside a congregation of the old faith, either from the beginning of the Reformation or in the course of its development. A third group of cities adopted the Reformation, either completely or in part, only to have it forcibly repressed. As far as I can see, of these 65 cities only 14 never officially tolerated a Protestant congregation within their walls during the sixteenth century, although most of these, too, had to deal at times with strong Protestant movements.

From B. Moeller: *Imperial Cities and the Reformation* (1972)

F The Spread of the Reformation in the Towns of Germany
Preaching and printed works - in whatever combination - soon began to have their effect on public opinion in the sophisticated German cities. Nuremberg, for instance, witnessed what historians have described as a massive outpouring of anticlerical sentiments. Evangelical ministers soon commandeered five of the town's churches, their efforts being ably seconded by the circulation of anonymous slander-sheets, and by monks who abandoned their cloisters to denounce the religious life. Traditional preachers were subjected to public criticism during celebrations of the Mass, and the old rites were

openly ridiculed in mock processions. It was therefore little surprise that when the laity presented demands for reform, as for instance in 1523 for communion in both kinds, the civic elite (many of whom had revealed early sympathy for the reform) were forced into a series of measures to rein in the evangelical movement and pre-empt more radical action. In 1525 the Reformation in Nuremberg was formally adopted. As in Nuremberg, so also in the other towns of Saxony, Franconia and the German south-west. In Strasburg a conservative council was forced to concede ever greater freedoms to a group of evangelical clergy supported by a substantial section of the city population. The reluctant endorsement of Martin Bucer's appointment as minister in August 1523 was followed in December by a decree that the town's ministers should teach nothing but the 'pure Gospel'. The speed of development depended to a large extent on the presence or absence of such charismatic local leaders, but even where there was no figure of stature the movement made steady progress through 1523 and 1524; this was the case at Frankfurt, Ulm and Augsburg, none of which yet formally adopted Reformation measures.

Thus, although it was only towards the end of the decade that the triumph of the Reformation achieved institutional confirmation in most German cities, it was clear that by 1525 the crucial transition towards the emergence of a popular movement had effectively been accomplished. In south Germany at least the movement had moved from its original epicentres, in monasteries and patrician and scholarly circles, towards being a coherent popular movement under clerical leadership.

From A. Pettegree: *The Early Reformation in Europe* (1992)

Questions

1 Why does the writer of Source A express some surprise at Luther's popularity? **(4 marks)**

2 Compare and contrast Sources B and C. In what ways do they differ in their explanations of Luther's popularity? Account for these differences. **(8 marks)**

3 Comment on the usefulness of polemical writings such as source D as a historical source. **(5 marks)**

4 From your own knowledge explain why Luther's message should have a particularly strong appeal in the towns. **(8 marks)**

5 'The Reformation was an urban event' (A.G. Dickens). Do Sources A-F support this view? **(10 marks)**

6 THE RADICAL REFORMATION IN GERMANY

There were signs of division and the emergence of a more radical reform movement than Lutheranism as early as 1522. Andreas Carlstadt was originally a prominent supporter of Luther. However, with Luther in hiding in the Wartburg and therefore temporarily off the scene, Carlstadt began to drive the progress of reform in Wittenberg in a noticeably radical direction. Carlstadt's iconoclasm, denial of the real presence and emphasis on the inner workings of the Spirit rather than the more objective Word (i.e. the Scriptures) were signs that all was not peace and harmony in the Lutheran camp. Luther was furious on his return to Wittenberg.

With the coming to prominence of Thomas Muntzer radicalism took on a new and violent edge. Muntzer had also been an early admirer of Luther but by 1524 he was much more mystical and apocalyptic in his emphasis. Most importantly, he began to advocate violence as a means of establishing the kingdom of God on Earth. The anarchic views of Muntzer and other anabaptists were a vital influence in the outbreak of the Peasants' War of 1524-5 for their preaching undoubtedly incited the violence.

The causes of the Peasants' War are rooted in the long-term socio-economic problems of fifteenth century German society, but how important were Luther's teachings as a catalyst and a theoretical justification for certain peasant demands? To some extent the authority of Scripture, justification by faith alone, the priesthood of all believers and, most importantly, Christian freedom provided ammunition for the peasant offensive against their lords. And what of Luther's response to the War? To begin with, he adopted a neutral, even-handed perspective, if anything favouring the peasants at the expense of the princes. Why, then, within a few weeks, did he come to condemn the peasants in no uncertain terms? Was he more disturbed by the threat of social disintegration or by the potential discrediting of his own cause? Finally, the importance of Luther's response to the War in determining the course of the Reformation in the countryside needs to be considered. To what extent did the peasantry feel betrayed by his *volte face?*

A Peasant Grievances

To the Christian reader, the peace and grace of God through Jesus Christ.
There are many antichrists who, now that the peasants are assembled

together, seize the chance to mock the gospel, saying, 'Is this the fruit of the new gospel: to band together in great numbers and plot conspiracies to reform and even topple the spiritual and temporal powers - yes, even to murder them?' The following articles answer all these godless, blasphemous critics. We want two things: first, to make them stop mocking the Word of God; and second, to establish the Christian justice of the current disobedience and rebellion of all the peasants.

The First Article

First of all, we humbly ask and beg - and we all agree on this - that henceforth we ought to have the authority and power for the whole community to elect and appoint its own pastor. We also want authority to depose a pastor who behaves improperly. This elected pastor should preach to us the holy gospel purely and clearly, without human additions or human doctrines or precepts. For constant preaching of the true faith impels us to get God for his grace, that he may instil in us and confirm in us that same true faith. Unless we have his grace in us, we remain mere, useless flesh and blood. For the Scripture clearly teaches that we may come to God only through true faith and can be saved only through His mercy. This is why we need such a guide and pastor; and thus our demand is grounded in Scripture.

The Second Article

Second, although the obligation to pay a just tithe prescribed in the Old Testament is fulfilled in the New, yet we will gladly pay the large tithe on grain - but only in just measure. Since the tithe should be given to God and distributed among his servants, so the pastor who clearly preaches the Word of God deserves to receive it.

The Third Article

Third, it has until now been the custom for the lords to own us as their property. This is deplorable, for Christ redeemed and bought us all with his precious blood, the lowliest shepherd as well as the greatest lord, with no exceptions. Thus the Bible proves that we are free and want to be free.

The Fourth Article

Fourth, until now it has been the custom that no commoner might catch wild game, wildfowl, or fish in the running waters, which seems to us altogether improper, unbrotherly, selfish and contrary to God's Word.

The Fifth Article

Fifth, we have another grievance about woodcutting, for our lords have seized the woods for themselves alone; and when the poor commoner needs some wood, he has to pay twice the price for it.

The Sixth Article

Sixth, there is our grievous burden of labour services, which the lords daily increase in number and kind. We demand that these obligations be properly investigated and lessened. And we should be allowed, graciously, to serve as our forefathers did, according to God's Word alone.

The Seventh Article

Seventh, in the future we will not allow the lords to oppress us any more. Rather, a man shall have his holding on the proper terms on which it has been leased, that is, by the agreement between lord and peasant.

The Eighth Article

Eighth, we have a grievance that many of us hold lands that are overburdened with rents higher than the land's yield. Thus the peasants lose their property and are ruined.

The Ninth Article

Ninth, we have a grievance against the way serious crimes are punished, for they are constantly making new laws.

The Tenth Article

Tenth, we have a grievance that some people have seized meadows and fields belonging to the community.

The Eleventh Article

Eleventh, we want the custom called death taxes totally abolished. We will not tolerate it or allow widows and orphans to be so shamefully robbed of their goods, as so often happens in various ways, against God and all that is honorable.

Conclusion

Twelfth, we believe and have decided that if any one or more of these articles is not in agreement with God's Word (which we doubt), then this should be proved to us from Holy Writ. We will abandon it, when this is proved by the Bible. If some of our articles should be approved and later found to be unjust, they shall be dead, null, and void from that moment on. Likewise, if Scripture truly reveals further grievances as offensive to God and a burden to our neighbour, we will reserve a place for them and declare them included in our list. We, for our part, will live and exercise ourselves in all Christian teachings, for which we will pray to the Lord God. For he alone, and no other, can give us the truth. The peace of Christ be with us all.

From the *Twelve Articles of the Peasantry,* February-March 1525

B Muntzer Stirs Up the Peasantry

May the pure fear of God be with you, dear brothers. How long are you going to slumber, how long are you going to resist God's will because, in your estimation, he has forsaken you? Ah, how often did I tell you that it had to be like this, that God cannot reveal himself in any other way, that you must remain unperturbed. If you fail to do so, then your sacrifice is in vain, your heart-sad, heart-felt suffering. You would then have to start suffering all over again. I tell you this, that if you are unwilling to suffer for the sake of God, then you will have to be martyrs for the devil. So watch out, don't be downcast, or negligent, or flatter any longer the perverted phantasts, the godless evil-doers; make a start and fight the fight of the Lord! It is high time; keep all your brothers at it, so that they do not scorn the divine testimony and perish as a result. The whole of Germany, France, Italy is awake; the master wants to set the game in motion, the evil-doers are for it. At Fulda four abbeys were laid waste during Easter week, the peasants in the Klettgau and the Hegau in the Black Forest have risen, three thousand strong, and the size of the peasant host is growing all the time. My only worry is that the foolish people will agree to a false treaty, because they do not yet realise the gravity of the situation.

Even if there are only three of you whose trust in God is unperturbable and who seek his name and honour alone, you need have no fear of a hundred thousand. So go to it, go to it, go to it! The time has come, the evil-doers are running like scared dogs! Alert the brothers, so that they may be at peace, and testify to their conversion. It is absolutely crucial absolutely necessary! Go to it, go to it, go to it! Show no pity, even though Esau suggest kind words to you, Genesis 33. Pay no attention to the cries of the godless. They will entreat you ever so warmly, they will whimper and wheedle like children. Show no pity, as God has commanded in the words of Moses, Deuteronomy 7; and he has revealed the same thing to us too. Alert the villages and towns and especially the mine-workers and other good fellows who will be of use. We cannot slumber any longer.

From a letter from Thomas Muntzer to the people of Allstedt, April 1525

C Luther's First Reaction to Peasant Unrest
To the Princes and Lords
We have no one on earth to thank for this disastrous rebellion, except you princes and lords, and especially you blind bishops and mad priests and monks, whose hearts are hardened, even to the present day. You do not cease to rant and rave against the holy gospel, even though you know that it is true and that you cannot refute it. In addition, as temporal rulers you do nothing but cheat and rob the people so that you may lead a life of luxury and extravagance. The poor people can bear it no longer. The sword is already at your throats ...

To make your sin still greater, and guarantee your merciless destruction, some of you are beginning to blame this affair on me and say that it is the fruit of my teaching ... You, and everyone else, must bear witness that I have taught with all quietness, have striven earnestly against rebellion, and have energetically encouraged and exhorted people to obey and respect even you wild and dictatorial tyrants. This rebellion cannot be coming from me. Rather the murder-prophets, who hate me as they hate you, have come along these people and have gone about among them for more than three years, and no one has resisted and fought them except me.

To the Peasants

So far, dear friends, you have learned only that I agree that it is unfortunately all too true that the princes and lords who forbid the preaching of the gospel and oppress the people unbearably deserve to have God put them down from their thrones (Lk. 1:52) because they have sinned so greatly against both God and man. And they have no excuse. Nevertheless, you, too must be careful that you take up your cause 'justly and with a good conscience ...'.

From Martin Luther: *Admonition to Peace* (March 1525)

D Luther Denounces the Peasants

In my earlier book on this matter, I did not venture to judge the peasants, since they had offered to be corrected and to be instructed; and Christ in Matthew 7 (:1) commands us not to judge. But before I could even inspect the situation, they forgot their promise and violently took matters into their own hands and are robbing and raging like mad dogs. All this now makes it clear they were trying to deceive us and that the assertions they made in their Twelve Articles were nothing but lies presented under the name of the gospel. To put it briefly, they are doing the devil's work. This is particularly the work of that archdevil who rules at Muhlhausen [Muntzer], and does nothing except stir up robbery, murder, and bloodshed; as Christ describes him in John (:44), 'He was a murderer from the beginning.' Since these peasants and wretched people have now let themselves be misled and are acting differently than they promised, I, too, must write differently of them than I have written, and begin by setting their sin before them, as God commands Isaiah (58:1) and Ezekiel (2:7), on the chance that some of them may see themselves for what they are. Then I must instruct the rulers how they are to conduct themselves in these circumstances.

The peasants have taken upon themselves the burden of three terrible sins against God and man; by this they have abundantly merited death in body and soul. In the first place, they have sworn to be true and faithful, submissive and obedient, to their rulers, as Christ commands when he says, 'Render to Caesar the things that are Caesar's' (Luke 20:25), and Romans 13 (:1) says, 'Let every person be subject to the governing authorities.'

In the second place, they are starting a rebellion, and are violently robbing and plundering monasteries and castles which are not theirs; by this they have doubly deserved death in body and soul as highwaymen and murderers.

Therefore let everyone who can, smite, slay and stab, secretly or openly, remembering that nothing can be more poisonous, hurtful, or devilish than a rebel. It is just as when one must kill a mad dog; if you do not strike him, he will strike you, and a whole land with you.

In the third place, they cloak this terrible and horrible sin with the gospel, call themselves 'Christian brethren', take oaths and submit to them, and compel people to go along with them in these abominations. Thus they become the worst blasphemers of God and slanderers of his holy name.

From Martin Luther: *Against the Robbing and Murdering Hordes of Peasants* (April - May 1525)

E A Popular Critique of Luther's Changing Views of the Peasant's War

From the title page of a pamphlet entitled *A Report on the Two false Tongues of Luther, how he Encourages the Peasants with one and Damns them with the other* (1525)

F   Violet Anticlericalism in Oberried Near Freiburg

On Wednesday after St Bartholomew's Day, [28 August] 1527 ... Blesy Krieg from Oberried confessed and testified freely and without constraint the following articles and points: Item, that he defected from his lordship to the peasants, thereby disregarding his honor and oath.

Item, in the peasants' rebellion he, along with others, entered the convent at Oberried, therein smashed the pyx containing the Host with a blacksmith's hammer, carried the Host to the altar in a monstrance, which he then also smashed; thereafter took the Host from the monstrance and laid it on the altar; apart from it there were five particles [of the Host] on a paten in a bag, which he took up to the altar and tipped out of the bag. Hans, Schilt's cowherd, Seger's maid, Michel Riegk's cowherd, these four, and he took the five particles, stuffed them in each other's mouths, he [Krieg] eating his. Thereupon he donned priest's robes, sang Mass, elevated the Host which he had removed from the monstrance in mockery and contempt, displayed it to the others, who had to ring the Sanctus bells, and set it down again. Then he consumed the Host in the manner of a priest; he spilled the chrism beside the altar; and Jacob Luttenschlager, Jacob Kunig, both from Todtnauberg, and Hans Klingle in the valley carried away a monstrance.

From the subsequent interrogation by the town council, 28 August 1527

G   Muntzer is Implicated by a Captured Peasant

... Was asked whom the congregation sent to the Muhlausen host at Volkenroda. Says, it was Claus Nickel that they sent there; he had brought a letter from the Muhlhausen host. The pastor of the congregation read out this letter on the meadow in front of the bakery. What he remembered of it was that Muntzer ordered them to tear down all the castles and homes of the nobility and to leave nothing standing. Secondly the letter included the statement that they should keep a close watch for the administrator, for the tyrant, the bloodhound, so that he did not escape from Salze, for things would not go well, if he got out of Salze; he should be struck dead.

From the interrogation of a captured peasant, 1525

H   A Catholic Perspective on the Causes of the Peasants' War

It can be concealed from no one that the origin of the peasant uproar, dissension, and affliction lies with the transgressions and oppressions of the clergy and nobility who have serfs. These they have burdened with unaccustomed grievances and have subjected them to intolerable coercion in many ways (about which, by the grace of God, we know very little), and have imposed upon them much which is neither proper, just godly, nor tolerable, as the cantons have informed me in their articles [i.e. those drawn up by the nine Catholic cantons at the

Confederate Diet at Lucerne on 2 February 1525]. As a result the cart is broken down, and the unwilling communities have slipped the harness ... which they have worn for so long. Those two cunning men, Luther and Zwingli, and their fellow sectaries were quite able to know and assess this, and were well informed why the common man was so recalcitrant ... Yes, it was a powerful weapon in their [the rebels'] arsenal that they [the preachers] constantly declared and pretended to the common man 'Christian freedom. Christian freedom; the hour has come when you will be saved and rid of your burdens if you so desire.' Certainly these were many grievances voiced against the prelates which were quite intolerable, and which should have been remedied and eased. But when one places a grievance in the hands of a madman, no one is thereafter his friend.

From Johannes Salat: *A sixteenth century Catholic Reformation Chronicle*

I   A Modern Historian's View of the Peasants' War

The evangelical message brought to this long tradition of peasant protest the sanction of a higher authority for their demands and grievances, the Word of God, a more concrete form of the 'divine law' to which they had sometimes appealed earlier. The Word of God as they understood it taught that serfdom was contrary to the freedom of Christians, that tithe was not justified in the Bible, and that any demands not founded on the Word of God should be held to be invalid.

Peter Blicke [see Source J] has seen the communal principle as so important for the reform movement that he speaks of a 'communal Reformation' (*Gemeindereformation*). The combination of evangelical ideas and communal principles was powerful enough to link together the differing interests of town and country into a potential revolution. The insistence on creating a true Christian community, based on principles of social justice founded in the Bible, was sufficiently subversive of a hierarchical feudal society to threaten its overthrow. As the Peasants' War gathered momentum in 1524-5, it seemed as though this revolution would indeed occur. The Twelve Articles, the main manifesto of the rebellious peasants, gave an ideological lead, and began to create an ideological unity over and above local allegiances.

The fate of the evangelical-social movements, with their idealistic proposals for radical social and religious reform, was largely sealed with the defeat of the Peasants' War. Both lay and clerical leaders of the evangelical movement tried even more ardently than some of them had before 1524 to detach religious reform from social protest. The rights of secular authorities were upheld by reformed preachers. Those preachers who were only mildly critical of secular authority, much less those with genuinely radical ideas, were quickly silenced or removed from their posts. The mayor of Zwickau, Hermann Muhlpfort, himself a determined opponent of disturbance, complained in 1525 that henceforth people would have to keep quiet on matters of injustice, or else risk being called rebellious.

From R. W. Scribner: *The German Reformation* (1987)

J Another Modern View of the War
Since it was the Reformation that gave revolutionary force to the rebellion of 1525, the Reformation itself could hardly remain unaffected by the peasants' military defeat. The most noticeable effect was a new concern for religious discipline on the part of the rulers. In the imperial abbey of Buxheim, a Carthusian house near Memmingen, for example, the abbot issued a new fundamental law in 1553. Its introduction stressed new rules about religion, laying various fines on those who stayed away from Mass or left church before it was over, gossiped during Mass, made fun of the pastor, violated the laws governing fasting, or refused Communion. The rules themselves were a direct response to the peasants' neglect of religion, or at least of the church, and were not just common places which crept more or less unintentionally into the territorial constitution. This is clear from the disproportionately high fines imposed: tithe refusal, for example, was punishable by ten gulden, the price of two or three cows.

The many new constitutions and police ordinances issued after 1525 confirm this impression, for they devote much attention to religion. Many foreshadow the Buxheim ordinance and reveal a general lack of popular interest in religion. These and similar sources support the view that after 1525 peasant attitudes towards 'the Reformation were indifferent, if not hostile.' Though often attacked, this hypothesis has never been convincingly refuted. Instead it has recently received support from the ranks of ecclesiastical historians, one of whom writes: 'Not only were the peasant revolts lost, but also the entire Reformation as a joint enterprise of laymen and clergy.'

From P. Blicke: *The Revolution of 1525* (1991)

Questions

1 What evidence is there in Source A of Luther's ideas influencing the peasants' demands?   **(5 marks)**

2 Compare and contrast Sources C and D. Account for Luther's changing views.   **(5 marks)**

3 How might Sources C and D account for peasant perceptions of Luther shown in Source F?   **(5 marks)**

4 From sources D, F and G and your own knowledge comment on the role of Muntzer and the radicals in the Peasants' War.   **(5 marks)**

5 Comment on the reliability and utility of Source H as an explanation of the causes of the Peasants' War.   **(5 marks)**

6 'A watershed in the history of the Reformation'. Do Sources A - J confirm this view of the Peasants' War?   **(10 marks)**

7 THE VISUAL PROPAGANDA
OF THE GERMAN REFORMATION

Recent historians, most notably Dr Bob Scribner, have sought to reduce the importance of the printed word as a means of communicating the Lutheran message, emphasising that only a tiny fraction - perhaps four or five per cent - of the population of the Empire could read. This has led to an interest in visual propaganda and, in particular, the woodcut. Yet if woodcuts were intended for an illiterate audience this does not mean that they are simple or easy to understand, particularly to a twentieth-century observer unfamiliar with the Scriptures which were the central frame of reference for Luther and his supporters.

The message of a woodcut such as Source J is self-evident - the papacy is diabolical in its origins and the artist illustrates this with a peculiarly crude ambiguity. One is left uncertain as to from which orifice the papacy is being produced. There is no great sophistication or theological awareness required here. Other woodcuts, however, are not so straightforward. In Source I we have four frames from a series of woodcuts comparing Christ and the Pope. The purpose is both polemical (provoking controversy) and didactic (instructive). The artist seeks to establish that the Pope, far from being the vicar of Christ as the Roman Church claimed him to be, was, in fact, the Antichrist prophesied by St. John in the Book of Revelation. He does this by comparing various episodes in the life of Christ taken from the Gospels with the contemporary conduct of the papacy. Thus the observer is both familiarised with the life of Christ and led to an inevitable conclusion as to the true nature of the papacy. Similar biblical knowledge is required to interpret Source K. Christ, according to St. John's Gospel, is the door of the sheepfold. Anyone who seeks to enter by another means is a thief and a robber. The enticements of the papacy and monks to enter the sheepfold by routes other than the door is proof that they are both erroneous and deceiving. Sources L, M and N are perhaps the most complex of all. These three woodcuts all have a common purpose, that of comparison between the Lutheran faith and Catholicism in order to promote the former and attack the latter. All three are packed full of biblical imagery and texts with Source M drawing heavily on St. Paul's teaching on spiritual warfare in Ephesians 6 and Source N on the contrasts between the Law and the Gospel made in the book of Romans.

Thus, perhaps it is not entirely accurate to view woodcuts as solely 'for the sake of simple folk'. Perhaps it would be more helpful to approach visual propaganda as an additional means of communicating the message of the Reformation to both literate and illiterate groups.

A Luther in 1519

¶ Getruckt zu Leypßgk durch Wolffgang Stöckl im iar.1519.

B Luther in 1520

C   Luther, inspired by the Holy Spirit

D   Luther as the Devil

E Luther's Heretical Game

F   Luther with Seven Heads

Sieben Köpffe Martini Luthers
Vom Hochwirdigen Sacrament des Altars / Durch
Doctor Jo. Cocleus.

Martinus Luther
Siebenkopff.

Doctor · Martino · Luther · Ecclesiast · Schwiemer · Visitirer · Barrabas

Fakſimile eines Flugblattes aus der Reformationszeit gegen Luther.

G   A Monk, Inspired by the Devil

H The Papal Ass

I Christ and Antichrist

Passional Christi vnd

Antichristi.

Er hat funden ym tepell vorkauffer/schaff/ochßen vñ tawben vñ wechßler sitzen/vñ hat glaich ein geyssel gamacht võ stricke alle schaff/ochßen/tauben vñ wechßler außen tempell trieben/das gelt verschüt/die ßall siede vmkart vñ zu den die tawben vorkaufften gesprochen. Hebt euch hin mit dißen auß mans vaters hauß solt ir nit ein kauff hauß mache. Joh.2. Ir habts vmb sunst/darüß gebts vmb sunst. Mat.10. Dein gelt sey mit dir yn vordamnuß. Act.8

Hie sitzt der Antichrist ym tempell gots vñ erzeygt sich alß got wie Paul' vorkündet 2. Theßal 2. vorandert alle göttlich ordnung wie Daniel sagt vnnd vnterdruckt die heylig schrifft/vorkaufft dispensacion/Ablas Pallia Bißthumb lehen/erhebt die schetz der erden/Loßt vff die ehe/beschwärt die gewißen mit seynen gesetzen/Macht recht vnd vmb gelt zureyßt er das/Ehbt heyligen/Benedeyet vñ maledeyet yns virde geschlecht vñ gebewt seyn tradicion gleych wie gots seyn c. sic. olis dis. 19. vnd nümants fall ym eynreden. 17 q. 4. c. nemini.

Passional Christi vnd

Antichristi.

In yrem ansehen ist er auffgehaben vnd die wolcken haben yhn hinwegt genommen võ yren augen. Diser Jesus der von euch yn hymmel auffgenommen ist/wirdt also wyder kommē wie yr yhn gesehen habt zu hymmel fharen. Act.1. Seyn reych hat keyn ende. Luce.1. Wer do mir dient der würd mir nach volgen vñ wu ich bin do wirt meyn diener auch seyn Joha.12.

Es ist agriffen die Bestia vñ mit yr õ falsch prophet der durch sie zeychen than hat do mit er vorfuret hat/die so seyn zeychē von yne genommen /vnd sein Bildt angebet seynt versenckt yn die teuffe des fewirs vnd schweffels vnd seynd getodt mit dem schwerdt des der do reydt vffen weyssen pferde/das auß seyne maul gehet. Apocal.19. Danne wirdt offenbar werden der schalckhafftige dem wirdt der herr Jesus toten mit dem atem seyns mundes vnd wirdt yn sturtzen durch die glori seyner zukunfft.2. ad Teßla.2.

J   The Origins of the Pope (1545)

ORTVS ET ORIGO PAPAE.

Hie wird geborn der Widerchrist/
Megera sein Seugamme ist/
Alecto sein Kindermeidlin/
Tisiphone die gengelt jn.

Mart. Luther D.
IX.   1545.

K   Christ's Sheepfold

L   Two Kinds of Preaching - The Evangelical and The Catholic

M The Battle Between the True Faith and False Spirituality

N The Law and the Gospel

Questions

1 From your own knowledge explain why so many woodcuts of Luther such as Sources A - C were made in the period 1519 - 21. **(4 marks)**

2 Compare and contrast Sources A - C with D - F. Account for their different perceptions of Luther. **(7 marks)**

3 How useful are polemics such as G - K as historical sources? Refer to the sources in your answer. **(7 marks)**

4 What messages are the artists seeking to communicate about the Catholic and Protestant faiths in Sources L - N? **(8 marks)**

5 'In an age of 5 per cent literacy the woodcut was the best way of communicating the Protestant message.' From Sources A - N and your own knowledge comment on this view. **(9 marks)**

8 LUTHERANISM OUTSIDE GERMANY

The controversies of 1517-21 thrust Luther not only onto the imperial stage but made him an internationally renowned figure. By 1521 admirers of Erasmus in the Netherlands were reading Luther and proclaiming boldly that the Christian humanist reform programme of their fellow countrymen had been strengthened considerably by events across the border in Germany. In France, too, reformers saw the work of humanist scholars such as Lefevre d'Etaples as being complemented by that of the Wittenberg reformer. Across the Channel, Cambridge University students were meeting to discuss Reformation theology at the White Horse tavern by 1525.

However, Lutheranism was ultimately a failure in the Netherlands, France and England alike. It was effectively crushed by central government. In the Netherlands, unlike Germany, Charles V was prince in his own right and thus rigorously imposed the Edict of Worms from its proclamation in 1521. The new faith had gained strong support in its earliest years from Luther's fellow Augustinians in Antwerp but, as early as 1523, two of these friars were burnt in Brussels, thus becoming the protomartyrs of the Reformation. By the following year Louis de Berquin, a French nobleman, was already running into trouble with the Sorbonne for possession of Luther's books. He was executed finally in 1529. Throughout the 1520s the French king Francis I was personally ambivalent towards the reform movement. He was sympathetic to Christian humanism but abhorred Lutheranism, yet at this stage it was far from clear where the former ended and the latter began. His hand was forced eventually by the anti-Catholic slogans of the Affair of the Placards in 1534. From this point on the Valois monarchy was steadfast in its resistance to reform. In England the opposition to Luther was apparent from 1521 when John Fisher, Bishop of Rochester, preached a sermon against him and Henry VIII published his defence of the seven sacraments.

Might Lutheranism have fared better in these states if Luther had offered a stronger lead? It is unlikely that resistance by force of arms would ever have been possible since the Lutherans were relatively few in number and, in any case, this was not something Luther was prepared to countenance. Even as late as 1530 he had theological difficulties with and sought to restrain the German princes in their struggle with Charles V. When the Schmalkaldic League was formed in 1531 it was only acceptable in Luther's eyes because its resistance to the Emperor came from those who were themselves appointed to positions of authority by God. Resistance by ordinary subjects was, for Luther, out of the question. The only practical alternative for evangelicals living in countries where the ruler was hostile, save that of emigration, was secret meetings known as conventicles. Yet, here again, Luther was unhappy. He associated conventicles with radicalism, anabaptism and schism. Their secret underground organisation ran counter to his vision of a reform of the entire Church. Does this explain why Lutheranism, although it made swift inroads into France, England and the Netherlands, particularly amongst the scholarly and intellectual elites, failed to take permanent root?

In Scandinavia the situation was entirely different. Here the Reformation flourished. Luther's books were in circulation in Sweden by 1524 and, although there were demands for suppression from the Church, the King, Gustavus Vasa, refused a ban. Three years later he granted Lutheranism free preaching and complete toleration. In Denmark, Norway and Finland there were similar, if somewhat later, moves to give the Reformation official state support. It is interesting to consider the extent to which the situation in Scandinavia paralleled that of Germany, and the extent to which secular authority was important to the success of Lutheranism. Were the motives of Scandinavian rulers in imposing a Reformation from above as mixed as the political and financial ambitions of the German princes; and could Lutheranism have been established without this princely backing?

A Early Support for the Reformation in the Netherlands

In the early 1520s the humanists were cock-a-hoop: obscurantism seemed at last to be in retreat and the Christian renaissance at hand. Cornelius Grapheus, the town secretary of Antwerp, rejoiced in 1521 that 'everywhere polite letters are being restored, the gospel of Christ has been re-born and Paul lives again'. To Grapheus, as to other humanists, it seemed as if the day prophesied by Joel (11:28) when the Lord would pour out his spirit 'upon all flesh', was about to be accomplished. In 1523 an unknown scholar at Groningen fervently hoped that many would turn at Easter 'from Aristotle to Paul, from Moses to Christ, from the Law to Grace, from the flesh to the spirit, from servitude to freedom and from fear to gladness'. This exultant mood soon faded. Grapheus and two fellow humanists from Antwerp had to recant their opinions in April 1522 and two Augustinian monks were burnt in Brussels in the summer of 1523.

From A.C. Duke: *Reformation and Revolt in the Low Countries* (1990)

B Coping with Persecution

... I wish you grace and peace in Christ, my venerable lord Doctor! There is being discussed amongst us the question of what a Christian ought to do about the taking of the Lord's Supper, whether it is permissible for him on his own behalf or that of a member of his family to call papal representatives [i.e. priests] to administer communion to him ... And since it greatly helps the consciences of the pious to have the testimonies of those who have been properly called to the preaching of the word of God, we beseech you by the flesh of Christ that you might be willing to indicate in a few words what we ought to do in this matter. Before now we have been accustomed to hold conventicles and in this way to celebrate the Lord's Supper, but it has been found that small profit ensues from this and many dangers and obstacles even amongst those devoted to the good news of Christ ... Hence it has happened that this question is being discussed amongst us, which we earnestly beseech you to solve for us!

From a letter to Luther from a follower in Antwerp, 1531

C The Prosecution of Louis de Berquin

Having attained the age of 40 years he had refrained from marrying, and such was his integrity and chastity that he was never burdened with any suspicion of moral turpitude, a remarkable state of affairs amongst courtiers. Before the Lord had called him to the knowledge of His Gospel he was quite openly a great interpreter of Papal decrees, great listener to masses and sermons and observer of fasts and feast days, as he had been since his youth. He was of a free and frank spirit and, as he had no wish to wrong anyone, he could also not bear wrong to be done to him. The teaching of Martin Luther, very new at that time in France was an absolute abomination to him, but being highly principled by nature, he also loathed the stupidity of the Sorbonnists and Monks, with the result that he often could not refrain, even among the most prominent in the kingdom, from voicing his true, sometimes, hostile, opinion of them.

Now, Berquin had engaged in some argument about a private dispute directed against one of the principals of the so-called Faculty of the Sorbonne, our master De Querca. This animosity resulting in his dedicating himself more and more closely to the contemplation of true piety, and the Lord looked kindly upon him, as He has His ways of drawing His followers to the knowledge of Jesus Christ, His only Son. From that time he constantly summoned every effort to employ himself in the reading of the Holy Scriptures and to translate Christian books from Latin into French. These he sent to his friends.

From these books the Sorbonnists found a way of extracting what they judged could enable them to distress Berquin and to subject him to their reproaches. In the manner of spiders they drew from his books several articles to make venom out of them and to bring about the death of a character who in integrity and breadth of mind strove to promote the doctrine of God. Typical of the articles was the following: that the Virgin Mary was wrongly invoked in sermons instead of the Holy Spirit; that for no reason she was called Treasurer of Grace: also that in the farewell or greeting rendered to her in the evening, contrary to all truth, she is called our hope, our life, all of which belongs to our Lord Jesus Christ alone.

For such and similar articles he was accused of heresy by the Sorbonne theologians, and at their insistence, put in prison.

From Jean Crespin's martyrology (1563 edition)

D Francis I Responds to the Protestant Challenge
Francis, by the grace of God etc ...

Since by the grace and mercy of God, our creator, the heresies and new sects contrary and damaging to the holy faith and catholic law of His church .... have ceased and are ceasing to exist, thanks in part to divine mercy and kindness and in part to the diligence we have applied and are applying under His authority in punishing in an exemplary manner many of the sectaries and imitators of the said errors ...

We say and declare by these presents that our will and intention is that those who are charged and accused of the said errors, as well as those who are under suspicion and not yet accused or prosecuted, should not be pursued or harassed on account of the said errors; but if they are held prisoner or their goods have been seized or confiscated, we want them to be delivered and set free and their goods to be returned to them in full.

And we allow exiles and fugitives to return to our said kingdom, countries, lands and lordships and to stay and live there in as much safety and freedom as they enjoyed hitherto, notwithstanding the banishments and confiscations of their persons and goods pronounced on account of their said contumacies.

Provided that they are bound to live as good and true Catholic Christians and desist from their said errors, which they will need to abjure canonically within the next six months, starting on the day of publication of these presents before their diocesans or their vicars and officials, and in the presence of the inquisitor of the faith or his vicar: provided also that if they return and relapse into crime they shall be punished strictly and harshly in accordance with the gravity of their offence.

And we do not intend Sacramentarians or those who have formally abjured in the past and have since lapsed to be included in these presents, but they are to be punished according to their faults. Furthermore, all are forbidden, on pain of hanging and of being held and reputed as rebels and disturbers of the public peace, to read, dogmatise, translate, compose or print, either publicly or privately, any doctrine contrary to the Christian faith.

From the edict of Coucy, July 1535

E   The Impact of Luther in Sweden
The Bishop, 21 May.

By the allegiance which I owe you, I deem it my duty to urge you not
to allow the sale of Luther's books within the realm, nor give his
pupils shelter or encouragement of any kind, till the coming council of
the Church shall pass its judgement ..... I know not how your Grace
can better win the love of God, as well as of all Christian Kings and
Princes, than by restoring the Church of Christ to the state of harmony
that it was enjoyed in ages past.

The King, 8 June.

Regarding your request that we forbid the sale of Luther's writings,
we know not by what right it could be done, for we are told his
teachings have not yet been found by impartial judges to be false.
Moreover, since writings opposed to Luther have been circulated
throughout the land, it seems but right that his too should be kept
public, that you and other scholars may detect their fallacies and show
them to the people. Then the books of Luther may be condemned. As
to your charge that Luther's pupils are given shelter at our court, we
answer that they have not sought it. If indeed they should, you are
aware it is our duty to protect them as well as you. If there be any in
our protection whom you wish to charge, bring your accusation and
give their names.

From the correspondence of Brask, Bishop of Linkoping, and Gustavus
Vasa, King of Sweden (1524)

F   The Impact of Luther in Denmark

1.   Henceforth every man shall enjoy freedom of conscience.
No one shall be at liberty to ask whether a man is Lutheran
or Catholic. Every man shall answer for his own soul.
2.   The King extends his protection to the Lutherans, who
hitherto have not enjoyed such full security and safe-
conduct as the Catholics.
3.   The marriage of ecclesiastics, canons, monks, and other
spiritual persons which for several centuries has been
forbidden, is now allowed; and every one is free to choose
whether he will marry or remain celibate.
4.   In future, bishops shall no more fetch the pall from Rome;
but after they have been duly elected by the chapters
possessed of the right, they shall seek confirmation from
the Crown.

From the Diet of Odense (1527)

G The Reform of the Church in Sweden

1. Vacancies in the parish churches are to be filled up by the bishop of the diocese. If, however, he appoints murderers, drunkards, or persons who cannot or will not preach the Word of God, the King may expel them and appoint other persons who are more fit.

2. Where a parish is poor, two of them may be joined together, though not if such a step would be an injury to the Word of God.

3. All bishops shall furnish the King with a schedule of their rents and income of every kind. From these schedules he shall determine the relative proportions for them to keep and to hand over to the Crown.

4. A similar course shall be pursued with regard to the cathedrals and chapters.

5. Auricular confession must be given up as already commanded, and an account must be rendered to the King of all fines imposed.

6. An account must also be rendered to the King of all fees received for remitting the ban, and bishops with their officers must not inflict the ban for petty offences, as has been often done hitherto.

7. Bishops shall have authority to determine as to the legality of marriages, and may grant divorces; but an account shall be rendered to the King of all fees therefor.

19. Fines for adultery and fornication belong to the King, not to the bishop.

20. The Gospel shall hereafter be taught in every school.

21. Bishops shall consecrate no priest who is incompetent to preach the Word of God.

22. No one shall be made a prelate, canon, or prebendary unless he has been recommended by the King, or his name submitted to the King.

From the Ordinances of Vasteras, 1527

Questions

1 From Source A and your own knowledge explain why Luther's ideas should be so well received in the Netherlands. **(6 marks)**

2 Comment on the reliability and utility of a martyrologist's account of an event such as source C. **(7 marks)**

3 What is at issue between the Bishop and the King in source F?
(3 marks)

4 Compare Sources F and G. To what extent are they influenced by Protestant ideas? **(7 marks)**

5 What light do Sources A - G shed on the reasons for the success and failure of the Reformation outside Germany? **(12 marks)**

9 LUTHER AND ZWINGLI: CONFLICT OVER THE LORD'S SUPPER

Historians used to believe that the Reformation in Zurich under Ulrich Zwingli was essentially borrowed from Luther and only began to diverge in 1524 over the issue of the real presence in the Eucharist. However, it is now recognised that Zwingli's reform movement was more or less independent from the start. Zwingli was always much more indebted to Christian humanism than his Wittenberg counterpart and between 1519 and 1522 he gradually drifted from an 'Erasmian' to a 'reformed' position whilst retaining his admiration for the Dutch scholar. It is important, then, to remember that the conflict over the Eucharist between Luther and Zwingli which culminated in the Colloquy of Marburg in 1529 was the product of two markedly different intellectual standpoints. Luther was, and in many ways always remained, a scholastic theologian, whereas Zwingli's thinking was shaped far more by the Renaissance.

In *The Babylonish Captivity of the Church* (1520) as well as his other early polemical and devotional tracts, Luther broke radically with Roman Eucharistic theology and practice. He rejected the Mass as a sacrifice and a good work, asserting that Christ's sacrifice upon the cross was eternally sufficient to forgive sins. Since he declared all Christians to be priests, Luther saw no justification for the denial of the chalice to the laity. He rejected transubstantiation as an explanation of how Christ is present in the bread and wine, declaring it to be a piece of thirteenth century scholastic nonsense. At one stage Luther even appeared to be moving towards a rejection of the real presence altogether, particularly emphasising the sacraments as a sign (see Sources B and C in Chapter 3). In the end, however, Luther stood by a literal interpretation of Christ's words at the last supper: 'This is My Body' and 'This is My Blood'.

Luther first came across a spiritual interpretation of the Eucharist and a denial of the real presence as early as 1522 through the somewhat idiosyncratic views of Andreas Carlstadt. For Carlstadt, when Christ spoke the words 'This is My Body', 'This' did not refer to the bread but to Christ's physical body, that is, Jesus was pointing not at the bread but at Himself. For Luther, this was lunacy and flew in the face of the plain text of Scripture. The episode is important, however, because thereafter *any* spiritual interpretation of the Eucharist was associated in Luther's mind with the fanaticism of Carlstadt. In 1524 Luther dismissed another somewhat more scholarly view, that of the Dutchman Cornelius Hoen, in

the form of a letter by Hoen brought to Wittenberg by one Hinne Rode.
For Hoen 'This *is* My Body' was best understood as 'This *signifies* My
Body'. Following a rebuff from Luther, Rode travelled to Basel,
Strasbourg and Zurich where he was much more warmly received.
Zwingli, like Luther, had rejected the sacrificial nature of the Mass but
now saw Hoen's view as the logical and rational interpretation of Christ's
words at the Last Supper and made them very much his own. It is no
coincidence that both Zwingli and Hoen were humanist scholars.

Was the Colloquy of Marburg organised by Philip of Hesse in 1529 was
doomed from the start? To what extent did the entrenched positions
adopted by Luther and Zwingli in the polemical battles of 1527-28 seal its
fate? How important was Luther's equating of Zwingli with the fanaticism
of Carlstadt? Philip of Hesse's aspirations should also be considered. Why
was he so anxious to secure a general evangelical alliance against Charles
V, and how did this relate to Luther's personal ambivalence over the
legitimacy of resistance? Another issue is the significance for Zwingli of
the failure to reach a consensus. To what extent did this failure
determine his diplomatic and military isolation which led to his defeat
and death at the second Battle of Kappel in October 1531?

A An Early Spiritual Interpretation of the Eucharist

Our Lord, Jesus Christ, promising many times to His own forgiveness
of sins and wishing to strengthen their souls at the Last Supper,
added a pledge to the promise lest there be any uncertainty on their
part; in the same way that a bridegroom who desires to assure his brid
e, lest she have any doubts, gives a ring to her saying 'Take this, I give
myself to you'. And she, accepting the ring, believes him to be hers
and turns her heart from all other lovers, and, to please her husband,
concentrates only on him. Just so he who takes the Eucharist - the
pledge of the Bridegroom which is proof of the giving of Himself -
ought steadfastly to believe Christ now to be his, given for him, and
His bloodshed for him ...

... If this consecrated bread is adored and honoured completely
like God but is not God, how, I ask you, are we any different from
those heathens who worship wood and stones? ... For the Lord
forbade us to believe them who said 'Here is Christ' or 'There is
Christ'; wherefore I should not have faith in those who say that Christ
is in the bread: for just this reason, I could not excuse myself as
having been deceived, since I have refused to listen to the warning
voice of Christ.

From a letter by Cornelius Hoen, c.1520-1

B Zwingli Adopts a Spiritualistic Interpretation

In the first article, God willing, it was made clear from the nature of
Christ's words that the saying: 'This is My Body,' cannot be taken

literally, otherwise we tear his flesh with our teeth in the very same way as it was pierced by the nails and the spear. In the second we considered the clear Scriptures which will not permit of the literal presence of his flesh and blood in this sacrament, a necessary procedure if we are not to rush to the details of the letter of Holy Scripture but in everything to test the meaning which Scripture as a whole will bear. For if Scripture is spoken by God, as is taught by Peter and Paul, then it cannot contradict itself. If it appears to do so, it is because we do not rightly understand it, comparing Scripture with Scripture. In this connection it has been made perfectly clear that the three articles of the Creed, 'He ascended into heaven, And sitteth on the right hand of God the Father Almighty; From thence he shall come to judge the quick and the dead' cannot be maintained if we accept the view that he is eaten in the body.

From Zwingli: *On the Lord's Supper* (1526)

C Luther Rejects Spiritualising Interpretations of the Lord's Supper

There are only three words; 'This is my body.' So the one (Carlstadt) turns up his nose at the word 'this' and severs it from the bread, claiming that one should interpret it thus; 'Take, eat, - this is my body'; as if I were to say: 'Take and eat; here sits Hans with the red jacket.' The second [Zwingli] seizes upon the little word 'is'; to him it is the equivalent of 'signifies'. The third [Oecolampadius] says, 'this is my body' means the same as, 'this is a figure of my body'. They set up these dreams of theirs without any scriptural basis. These fanatics do not disturb me, and are not worthy that one should fight with them. Some of them are crude, grammatical fanatics; the others are subtle, philosophical fanatics. Let them go, therefore, and let us adhere to the words as they read: that the body of Christ is present in the bread and that his blood is truly present in the wine. This does not mean that he is not present in other places also with his body and blood, for in believing hearts he is completely present with his body and blood. But it means that he wishes to make us certain as to where and how we are to lay hold of him. There is the Word, which says that when you eat the bread you eat his body, given for you. If the Word were not there, I would not pay any heed to the bread. Let this suffice for the first part.

From Martin Luther: *The Sacrament of the Body and Blood of Christ - Against the Fanatics* (1526)

D Dialogue over the Lord's Supper

Nevertheless, they desired that first of all there be a discussion of the Lord-Supper for that was why this meeting had been arranged; after this had been finished all the remaining items could ... be discussed.

Luther agreed to this procedure, but protested that he did not agree with the writings of these people. He desired to indicate this disagreement so that people at home might not say that he was not allowed to speak freely. He went on to cite their basic principles :

1. they desire to prove their case by way of logical conclusions;
2. they hold that a body cannot be in two places at the same time and that it cannot be infinite;
3. they appeal to natural reason.

I do not ask how Christ can be God and man and how these natures could be united, for God is able to do more than anything we can imagine. We must submit to the word of God. They themselves must prove that the body of Christ is not there [when Christ himself says]: 'This is my body.' He does not want to hear what reason says. He rejects entirely human arguments like the geometrical argument that a gate cannot fit into a doorway, nor can a post fit into a hole the size of a finger. Therefore, he requests a valid proof.

Oecolampadius, responding to the arguments of Luther, said: Chapter 6 [of St. John's Gospel] explains the other passages of Scripture. Christ is not present there [i.e. in the sacrament] locally. He [Oecolampadius] did not want to appeal to reason or geometry, but because he possessed the fullness of faith he spoke on the basis of [such a] faith, for Christ has risen. Our opinion is neither new nor profane.

From The *Marburg Colloquy* (1529)

E   The Consequences of the Failure to Reach Agreement at Marburg
The dispute between Luther and Zwingli is important at both the theological and political levels. At the theological level, it raised the gravest of doubts concerning the principle of the 'clarity of scripture'. Luther and Zwingli were unable to agree on the meaning of such phrases as 'this is my body' (which Luther interpreted literally, and Zwingli metaphorically) and 'the right hand of God' (which - with apparent inconsistency on both sides - Luther interpreted metaphorically and Zwingli interpreted literally). The exegetical optimism of the early Reformation may be regarded as foundering on this rock: scripture, it seemed, was far from easy to interpret.

At the political level, the dispute ensured the permanent separation of the two evangelical factions of the Reformation. An attempt to mediate between their rival views took place at the Colloquy of Marburg (1529), attended by such luminaries as Bucer, Luther, Melanchthon, Oecolampadius and Zwingli. By this stage, it was increasingly obvious that unless the Reformation could achieve a significant degree of internal unity, at least some of its gains would be reversed. The catholics had been inhibited from taking military action against the cities of the Reformation due to such long-standing disputes as that between Emperor Charles V and Francis I of France on the one hand, and Pope Clement VII on the other. In 1529, these disputes were resolved within weeks of each other. Suddenly, the two wings of the Reformation faced a powerful political and military threat. The most obvious course of action was to settle their differences - a procedure urged by Bucer, who suggested that differences should be tolerated among evangelicals, provided they agreed to recognise the Bible alone as the normative source of faith. The Protestant landgrave Philip of Hesse, anxious at the new political situation, brought Luther and Zwingli together in the castle hall of Marburg in an attempt to resolve their differences.

That attempt foundered on one point and one point only. On fourteen articles, Luther and Zwingli felt able to agree. The fifteenth had six points, on which they were able to reach agreement on five. One point, and one point only, remained. But for Luther, Christ was really present at the eucharist, whereas for Zwingli he was present only in the hearts of believers. Philip of Hesse's hope of a united evangelical front against the newly-regrouped catholic forces was dashed and the political credibility of the Reformation seriously compromised. By 1530, Charles V had begun to re-assert his authority over the German Reformation, helped to no small extent by the political consequences of the differences between Luther and Zwingli over the eucharist.

From A. E. McGrath: *Reformation Thought: an Introduction* (1988)

F   The Eucharistic Debate After Marburg
The unresolved debate between Zwingli and Luther was not the end of the story. The German (as opposed to Swiss) reformed cities could not indefinitely remain estranged from the Lutheran churches. As early as the 'Four Cities' Confession' (Confessio Tetrapolitana) produced by the 'Zwinglian' cities of Strasbourg, Constance, Lindau, and Mem-mingen at the Augsburg Reichstag in 1530, it was affirmed that 'true body and true blood' were 'truly eaten and drunk', not mere bread and wine. Between March and May 1536 Bucer (for the south Germans) and Luther, Melanchthon, and Bugenhagen negotiated the 'Wittenberg accord'. Amongst other issues, this accord stated that body and blood were 'truly and substantially' present and received in the Eucharist. It allowed the full political (and later doctrinal) unity between north and south Germany which had been so elusive seven years before. Switzerland, too, saw shifts in Eucharistic teaching. In Calvin's hands Luther's and Zwingli's positive emphases, without their destructive elements, were reconciled into a complete system. On one hand Calvin taught that Christ's 'fleshly' presence was a reassurance

of his closeness; his 'flesh and blood' fed the soul as food and drink fed the body; Christ penetrated into the believer's 'bones and marrow'. On the other he agreed with Zwingli that 'this is my body' was figurative, a metonymy: Christ's body was not 'physically' present in a gross sense. Believers were lifted up spiritually to Christ; he was not dragged down 'bodily' to them. On this basis, Calvin's allies Theodore de Beze and Guillaume Farel (who had earlier taught an even more extreme rejection of the physical presence of Christ than Zwingli) could claim that their beliefs on the Eucharist were essentially those of the Lutherans.

From E. Cameron: *The European Reformation* (1991)

Questions

1 What arguments are used by Hoen in Source A to oppose the real presence? **(4 marks)**

2 Compare and contrast Zwingli's and Luther's views of the Eucharist in B and C. **(7 marks)**

3 Comment on the purpose and tone of Source C. **(6 marks)**

4 From Source D and your own knowledge explain the points of agreement and the points at issue at the Colloquy of Marburg.
(6 marks)

5 Look at Sources A - F. How significant was the eucharistic controversy in limiting the success of the Reformation? **(12 marks)**

Specimen answers to these questions can be found on pages 99-101.

10 CALVIN'S EARLY LIFE

As Alistair McGrath, one of Calvin's most recent biographers, has pointed out, we know remarkably little about Calvin's early life. Luther wrote a huge amount in the crucial period from 1517 to 1521. Indeed, his celebrity status was to a large extent based on his skills as a writer, whereas Calvin put pen to paper very rarely in the early 1530s. Luther gives us much autobiographical information later in life, but Calvin's personal modesty prevented him from doing likewise and he has left us with only a few lines from the preface to his *Commentary on the Psalms* (1557). Finally, Calvin's early biographers are far from neutral. Jerome Bolsec on the one hand is unbelievably hostile and Theodore Beza is the exact opposite. Thus, although we are left with a reasonable biographical sketch of Calvin's formative years, we have very little knowledge of his spiritual development.

Born at Noyon in Picardy in 1509, Calvin's early life was conventional enough. He studied at Paris, Orleans and Bourges universities between 1523 and 1531 and under the direction of his father, appeared destined for a career in the Law. By the time of his return to Paris in 1531, Calvin had already come under the influence of Christian humanism, which was strong in French intellectual and even royal circles in the 1520s. Thus in 1532 it came as no surprise that his first book was a commentary on Seneca's *De clementia,* a standard task befitting an ambitious and gifted young humanist. However, Calvin in 1533, whilst still in all probability only a Christian humanist rather than a thorough-going reformer, Calvin ran foul of the Sorbonne, the Faculty of Theology at the University of Paris. On 31 October Nicolas Cop, the newly elected rector of the university and a personal friend of Calvin, delivered an address. It was a mixture of traditional Catholicism and Christian humanism tinged with a little Lutheranism, but it aroused strong emotions and Cop was summarily dismissed from his post. As a known humanist and friend of Cop, Calvin was implicated (indeed he may have even written the sermon) so he decided to quit Paris. Within seven months his transition from pious Catholic to 'reformed' appears to have been complete for in May 1534 he wrote to Noyon Cathedral resigning the benefices his father had purchased in 1521 to enable him to study. By the time of the Affair of the Placards (see Chapter 8), Calvin knew there could be no compromise. Calvin was later to describe himself as undergoing a 'sudden conversion', but it is difficult to marry this reminiscence with what appears to be the gradual development of his views. We must ask ourselves to what extent Calvin's mind was made up for him by the increasingly hostile stance in France towards religious innovation - whether of a Christian humanist or of a Lutheran variety. It is possible that 'sudden conversion' might have been more of a literary device by which Calvin allied himself to other great saints, such as St Paul whom God set aside for specific tasks. This would concur with the sense of mission permeating Calvin's life from 1536 onwards.

A   Calvin's Early Life.

He was born in Noyon, an ancient and famous town of Picardy, the year 1509, the tenth of July, of an honest house and of a reasonable wealth, his father was named Gerard Calvin, a man of good under-standing and counsel, and therefore greatly desired in the houses of noble men dwelling in those parts: by reason whereof his said son was the better and more liberally brought up, at his father's charges notwithstanding, in company with the children of the house of Montmor, with whom he was also in company at the school in Paris.

He was always a singular good wit and above all other things of a very good conscience, enemy to vices, and greatly given to the service of God as men did then call it: in such sort as his mind was wholly to divinity, which was also an occasion that he was provided of a benefice in the Cathedral Church of Noyon.

Yet was his father always minded that he should study the Laws, and he also on his part having already (by the mean of a cousin and friend of his, named Master Pierre Robert, otherwise Olivetanus, who afterwards turned the Bible out of Hebrew into French and imprinted it at Neuchatel) tasted something of the pure Religion, began to withdraw himself from the popish superstitions: which was the cause that beside the singular reverence that he had towards his father, he did agree to go to Orleans to the same end, where there did then read an excellent man named Pierre de l'Estoile, who was afterwards President of the Court of the Parlement in Paris, under whom he did so profit in short space, that he was not accounted a scholar, but an ordinary Doctor, as often times he was rather a teacher than a hearer, and he was offered to proceed Doctor without paying anything, which thing also he did refuse.

[Calvin studied briefly in Bourges.] Among other with whom he did frequent and company then at Bourges there was … an excellent personage, a professor of the Greek tongue, named Melchior Wolmar … This good man seeing Calvin not to be well instructed in the Greek tongue, caused him to study the same, wherein he did greatly help him, as he himself hath witnessed, dedicating to him his commen-taries upon the Second Epistle of St Paul to the Corinthians, and did him the honour to call him his Master and instructor.

In the meantime his father died, which was the cause that he left the study of the Laws and returned to Noyon, and then to Paris: where notwithstanding his youth, he was not long unknown nor without honour, by all such as had any feeling of the truth: he of his part did then resolve to dedicate himself wholly to God, and did travail with great profit in such sort, that being in Paris at the time of the Rector named Monsieur Cop, there happened a sedition ... In the end seeing the miserable estate of the realm of France, he determined to absent himself and to be where he might live more quietly and according to his conscience.

From a late sixteenth-century account of Calvin's life by his successor, Theodore Beza

B Calvin's Conversion
So it came to pass that I was withdrawn from the study of arts and was transferred to the study of law. I endeavoured faithfully to apply myself to this, in obedience to my father's wishes. But God, by the secret hand of his providence, eventually pointed my life in a different direction.

At first, I was so obstinately devoted to the superstitions of the Papacy (and more stubbornly so than was right for someone of my age) that I was not easily extricated from so profound an abyss. Then God, by a sudden conversion, changed and shaped my heart towards being more receptive. Having received some taste and inkling of the true piety, I was immediately stirred up to enthusiasm for it and, although I did not immediately put to one side all my other studies, I pursued them more spasmodically. But I was amazed to discover that, within a year, all those around with a similar yearning for the pure doctrine, came to me for assistance, even though I was only a novice myself. For my part, being rather shy and preferring tranquillity and repose, I began to look for some quiet retreat from them. But, no sooner had I found what I wanted than, on the contrary, these places of retreat turned into public schools. Despite my wish always to live in obscurity and retirement, God so moved and transformed me through a variety of experiences and never left me in peace anywhere until, contrary to my natural inclinations, he brought me towards enlightenment and, so to speak, forced me into the open.

From Jean Calvin: *Preface to the Commentary on the Book of Psalms* (1557)

C Calvin is Implicated in Heresy
At this time Nicolas Cop, son of Guillaume Cop of Basel, physician to the king, had been appointed rector in the university of Paris. According to the custom, he had to deliver an oration on 1 November, the feast of All Saints' Day to the papists, and Calvin provided him with a sermon in which religion was dealt with more trenchantly and

with greater purity than had generally been the case in the past. This
was intolerable to the Sorbonne and also disapproved of by the
Senate or Parlement, which called the rector to appear before it. He
accordingly set out with his officers but, being warned on the way to
take heed of his enemies, he turned back home and afterwards left the
country and retired to Basel. Searches were made at the college of
Fortret where Calvin happened to be residing. He was not at home but
his papers were seized and, amongst them, numerous letters from his
friends. Worst of all, this gravely endangered the lives of many of
them, for these judges were very harsh against the Church, especially
one of them called Jean Morin, whose savage proceedings are
well-remembered. This tempest the Lord dispersed by means of the
queen of Navarre, only sister to King Francis, a woman of admirable
intelligence and, at this time, a patroness of the Reformers. Inviting
Calvin to her court, she received him and listened to him with the
greatest respect.

From Theodore Beza: *Life of Calvin* (1564)

D The Religious Climate in Paris in 1533
As October 1533 drew to a close, there were thus conflicting signals to
be observed concerning the climate for reform at Paris. The faculty of
theology retained its former hostility, whether to Lutheranism or
humanism; its power, however, seemed temporarily to have been
reduced. The king, on the other hand, perhaps increasingly inclined to
take account of the pro-evangelical views of Marguerite of Navarre,
seemed well disposed towards the moderate reformist views
associated with Lefevre d'Etaples and his disciples, such as Roussel.
These men, although clearly passionately concerned for the spiritual
state of the catholic church, saw themselves as called to renew it from
within; they were not 'reformers' as that word would later be
understood. It was perhaps easy for those sympathetic to the cause of
reform to be seduced by such positive signs, and overlook more
ominous indicators suggesting the climate was hardening against the
evangeliques. Nicolas Cop, newly elected as rector of the University of
Paris in the autumn of 1533, chose to devote his inaugural address to
the need for reform and renewal within the church. It was to prove a
catastrophic error of judgement.

From A.E. McGrath: *A Life of John Calvin* (1990)

Questions

1 'Greatly given to the service of God' (source A) and 'obstinately
devoted to the superstitions of the Papacy' (source B). Is it possible

to reconcile these two statements on Calvin's early life? **(8 marks)**

2 How reliable are Calvin's autobiographical remarks in source B?
(8 marks)

3 From source C and your own knowledge explain why Calvin left France in 1533. **(5 marks)**

4 'Catholic', 'humanist', 'evangelical', 'Protestant'. Study sources A-D and assess which label is the most fitting for Calvin up to 1533.
(14 marks)

11 CALVIN THE RELIGIOUS THINKER - THE *INSTITUTES*

Calvin's reputation as a theologian does not rest on the *Institutes* alone. He was a prolific preacher, a biting polemicist and a weighty biblical commentator and this chapter contains examples of such writings. Yet his significance as a theologian depends first and foremost on his *magnum opus,* the *Institutes of the Christian Religion.* First published in Basel in 1536 the *Institutes* was essentially a catechism based on Luther's *Short Catechism* of 1529. It contained six chapters on the Ten Commandments, the Apostles' Creed, the Lord's Prayer, the Sacraments, the 'False' Sacraments and Christian Liberty. In addition, it included a preface addressed to King Francis I which emphasised the biblical and reasonable nature of French evangelicalism to distinguish it from the lunatic fringe anabaptist kingdom of Munster which had collapsed only a year earlier. By the time of the second edition of 1539, the *Institutes* had been expanded threefold and comprised 17 chapters. Already it was no longer merely a catechism but a guide to Scripture. By 1553 the Institutes had been divided up into four books dealing with God the Father, Christ, the work of the Holy Spirit and the Church and the Sacraments. It reached its final and definitive form in 1559 by which time it had become a training manual for prospective Reformed ministers. Between 1536 and 1599 the *Institutes* was published at least 52 times and translated from Latin into six other languages - French, Italian, Dutch, English, German and Spanish.

The central themes of the *Institutes* are the glory of God and the divinity of Christ. God, for Calvin, can only be known through the Scriptures by the relation which comes through the Holy Spirit. Both the Old and New Testaments reveal Christ, the former foreshadowing the latter. It must be noted that the doctrine of predestination did not feature particularly strongly in the *Institutes.* Why, then, did it achieve such pre-eminence after Calvin's death? The doctrine achieved a higher profile in later editions of the *Institutes,* and its greater emphasis may be somewhat polemical in purpose and be linked to its coming under attack from Calvin's opponents. How significant was its positioning, and why did it follow Calvin's discussion on grace and justification when it would have been more logical for it to have preceded these topics? Calvin's purpose in teaching this doctrine should also be considered: was it for theological speculation or was it for the assurance and comfort of the believer?

A On Images and Idolatry

Second Commandment: You shall not make a graven image for yourself nor any likeness of things which are in heaven above, or on earth beneath, or in the waters under the earth; and you shall not adore or worship them (Ex. 20: 4-5).

This means: all worship; and adoration is owed to the one God. He is incomprehensible, incorporeal, invisible, and so contains all things that he can be enclosed in no place. Let us then fervently pray against our imagining he can be expressed in any figure, or represented in any idol whatsoever, as if it were God's likeness. Rather, we are to adore God, who is Spirit, in spirit and in truth (Dt. 6: 13-16; 1: 12-13; 1 Kings 8: 22-27; 1 Tim. 1: 17; Jn. 1: 9-14; 4:24). The First Commandment therefore teaches that there is one God, apart from whom no other gods are to be thought of or held to. This commandment teaches God himself is such and is to be honored by such worship that we dare not attach anything physical to him, or subject him to our senses, as if he could be comprehended by our dull heads, or be represented in any form.

Those who are trying, with a miserable excuse, to defend an accursed idolatry that many ages ago had swamped and sunk true religion, should attend to this. Images, they assert, are not to be taken for gods. Not so utterly unthinking were the Jews as to forget it was God by whose hand they had been led out of Egypt, before they fashioned the calf. Not so senseless are we to deem the gentiles as not to have understood God to be something else than wood or stones ...

The ultimate evasion is that they call them "the books of the uneducated". Suppose we grant this (although it is completely vain, since it is more than certain, that the only purpose for prostration is to worship) - I still cannot see what benefit such images can provide for the unlearned (especially for those for whom they wish to portray God) except to make them into anthropomorphites. The things they dedicate to saints -what are they but examples of the most abandoned lust and obscenity? If anyone wished to model himself after them, he would be fit for the lash. Indeed, brothels show harlots clad more virtuously and modestly than the churches show those objects which they wish to be seen as images of virgins. Therefore let them compose their images at least to a moderate decency, that they may with a little more modesty falsely claim that these are books of some holiness!

But then we shall also answer that this is not the method of teaching the people of God whom the Lord wills to be instructed with a far different doctrine than this trash. He has set forth the preaching of his Word as a common doctrine for all. What purpose did it serve for so many crosses - of wood, stone, even of silver and gold - to be erected, if this fact had been duly and faithfully taught: that Christ was offered on account of our sins that he might bear our curse and cleanse our trespasses? From this one word they could have learned more than from a thousand crosses of either wood or stone. For perhaps the covetous fix their minds and eyes more tenaciously upon gold and silver than upon any word of God.

From Jean Calvin: *Institutes of the Christian Religion* (1536)

B   The Relationship Between Scripture and the Holy Spirit
By this one word we may refute all the inventions which Satan has brought into the Church from the beginning under the pretended authority of the Spirit. Mohammed and the Pope have this religious principle in common, that scripture does not contain the perfection of doctrine, but that something higher has been revealed by the Spirit. The Anabaptists and Libertines have in our own day drawn their madness from the same ditch. But the spirit which introduced any invention foreign to the gospel is a deceiver and not of Christ; for Christ promises the Spirit who will confirm the teaching of the gospel as if he were signing it.

From Jean Calvin: *Commentary on the Gospel of John*

C   On Foreknowledge
The decree, I admit, is a fearful one; and yet it is impossible to deny that God foreknew what the end of man was to be before he created him, because he had so ordained by his decree. If anyone inveighs at the point against the foreknowledge of God, he does so rashly and thoughtlessly. Why indeed should the heavenly judge be blamed because he was not ignorant of what was to happen? If there is any just or plausible complaint it applies to predestination. It ought not indeed to seem ridiculous for me to say that God not only foresaw the fall of the first man and in him the ruin of his posterity, but also brought it about in accordance with his own will. For as it belongs to his wisdom to know beforehand everything that is to happen, so it belongs to his power to rule and direct everything by his hand.

From Jean Calvin: *Institutes* (1559)

D   On Predestination and Election
In actual fact, the covenant of life is not preached equally amongst all men, and amongst those to whom it is preached it does not gain the same acceptance either constantly or in equal degree. In this diversity, the wonderful depth of God's judgement is made known to us. For there is no doubt that this variety also serves the decision of God's eternal election ... This seems a baffling question to men. For they think nothing more inconsistent than that out of the common multitude of men some should be predestined to salvation, others to

73

destruction. But it will become clear that they are needlessly entangled ... for we shall never be clearly persuaded, as we ought to be, that our salvation flows from the wellspring of God's free mercy until we come to know his eternal election, which illumines God's grace by this contrast: that he does not indiscriminately adopt all into the hope of salvation but gives to some what he denies to others ...

As scripture clearly shows, we say that God established by his eternal and unchangeable plan those who he long before determined once for all to receive into salvation, and those whom, on the other hand, he would devote to destruction. We assert that, with respect to the elect, this plan was founded upon his freely given mercy without regard to human worth; but, by his just and irreprehensible judgement, he has barred the door or life to those whom he has given over to damnation.

From Jean Calvin: *Institutes* (1559)

E An Interpretation of the Eucharist

Now, if it be asked whether the bread is the body of Christ and the wine his blood, we answer, that the bread and the wine are visible signs, which represent to us the body and blood, but that this name and title of body and blood is given to them because they are as it were instruments by which the Lord distributes them to us. This form and manner of speaking is very appropriate. For as the communion which we have with the body of Christ is a thing incomprehensible, not only to the eye but to our natural sense, it is there visibly demonstrated to us. Of this we have a striking example in an analogous case. Our Lord, wishing to give a visible appearance to his Spirit at the baptism of Christ, presented him under the form of a dove. St. John the Baptist, narrating the fact, says, that he saw the Spirit of God descending. If we look more closely, we shall find that he saw nothing but the dove, in respect that the Holy Spirit is in his essence invisible. Still, knowing that this vision was not an empty phantom, but a sure sign of the presence of the Holy Spirit, he doubts not to say that he saw it (John 1: 32), because it was represented to him according to his capacity.

From Jean Calvin: *A Short Treatise on the Lord's Supper* (1540)

Questions

1 On what basis in Source A does Calvin reject the generation of images? **(3 marks)**

2 What, according to Calvin in Source B, do Moslems, Catholics and Anabaptists all have in common? **(3 marks)**

3 Compare the arguments used in Sources C and D. Is it possible to distinguish between Calvin's doctrines of foreknowledge, predestination and election? **(6 marks)**

4 From Sources A, C and D and your own knowledge comment on the contrasting styles of the first and final editions of the Institutes.
(6 marks)

5 Compare Source E with Sources B, C and F in Chapter 9. In what ways does Calvin's interpretation of the Lord's Supper differ from that of Luther and Zwingli? **(8 marks)**

6 Study Sources A - E. To what extent do they demonstrate Calvin to be a 'biblical theologian'? **(9 marks)**

12 CALVIN THE PRACTICAL REFORMER - GENEVA

Calvin first arrived in Geneva in August 1536. He was expecting only to stay overnight on his way to Strasbourg. However, Geneva had become a Protestant city only a mere three months earlier and when he arrived he found a state of religious chaos. Calvin would have been far happier continuing with his scholarly pursuits but he was pressurised to stay by Guillaume Farel who, until this point, had led the cause of reform in Geneva, but recognised his own lack of organisational ability.

Calvin enjoyed a far from easy time in Geneva. His first stay lasted less than two years for, in April 1538, he and Farel were banished from the city after a sharp disagreement with the magistrates as to who should exercise control of the Church. For the next three years, Calvin spent a happy and fruitful spell in Strasbourg, working under the leadership of Martin Bucer. In 1541 Calvin was invited back to Geneva and returned reluctantly but in a somewhat stronger position. His *Ecclesiastical Ordinances* of November 1541, which bear the influence of Bucer and his sojourn in Strasbourg, became the model for church government in Geneva for the rest of his life. However, Calvin, at least until 1555, enjoyed a somewhat tense and uneasy relationship with Geneva's magistrates. Whilst it was recognised that Calvin was needed to lead the Genevan Church, he was disliked and mistrusted as a foreigner and the magistrates were extremely reluctant to concede him any of their power.

From that point until his death in 1564, Calvin was able to dominate Geneva. How was he able to do this? To what extent did Calvin's strength lie in his office as a pastor, and how much of his power rested on his own personality? Other issues should be considered, such as why Geneva tolerated Calvin's 'dictatorship'; the effects of his ministry on the city and on Geneva's status in the Europe of the later sixteenth century; and the importance of the creation of the Genevan Academy (an international training college for Protestant ministers) and the Consistory in enhancing Geneva's reputation. Should Calvin claim the credit for establishing Geneva as the chief Protestant city of Europe, and what benefits did he bring the city?

It was perhaps the Consistory which was Calvin's most important contribution to the success and spread of the Reformation. In the *Ecclesiastical Ordinances* of 1541 Calvin, borrowing from Bucer, had established a fourfold ministry for the Church in Geneva - pastors, teachers, elders and deacons - the latter two offices being reserved for the laity. The Consistory was made up of pastors and elders and thus contained a balance of ministers and lay persons. In fact, Calvin struggled for most of his career to increase the number of ministers in the Consistory and thereby wrestle control of the Genevan Church away from the magistrates. This was not achieved decisively until the very end of his life. The Consistory met every Thursday and had the task of maintaining Church discipline. It had no secular power, but rather its task was to deal with sin, since for Calvin purity in the Church was of crucial importance. Thus, it would hear cases on fornication, adultery, blasphemy, drunkenness, wife-battering and the like. The most serious sentence which could be imposed was that of excommunication - a ban on taking communion at the next quarterly service. Why was the Consistory a model adopted all over Europe? How was Calvin able to create a body flexible enough to appeal to princes and magistrates as a tool of social control and equally effective where rulers opposed Reformed Protestantism and forced it underground?

A Calvin's Arrival in Geneva (1536)

Wherever I went, I took care to conceal that I was the author of the *Institutes* and resolved to retain my privacy and obscurity. At length, Guillaume Farel detained me in Geneva, not so much by counsel and exhortation, as by a dreadful threat which I felt in the same way as if God had laid his mighty hand upon me from heaven to arrest me. As the most direct road to Strasbourg, to which I then intended to retire, was shut by the wars, I decided to go quickly via Geneva, not intending to spend longer than a single night in the city. A little before this, popery had been driven from the place by the exertions of that excellent man whom I have just mentioned and Pierre Viret. But matters were not yet settled there and the city was divided into ungodly and dangerous factions. Then a person ... discovered who I was and made me known to the rest . Upon this, Farel, who was consumed with an extraordinary zeal to advance the gospel, immediately strained every nerve to detain me. And, after learning that my heart was set upon devoting myself to private studies, for which I wished to keep myself free from other pursuits, and, finding that he achieved nothing by his entreaties, he proceeded to warn me that God would curse my retirement and the tranquillity which I sought for my studies if I withdrew and refused to help when it was so urgently needed. By this I was so struck with terror that I gave up the journey I had planned to undertake. But, aware of my natural shyness, I refused to tie myself to any particular position.

From Jean Calvin: *Commentary upon the Psalms* (1557)

B Calvin is Banished from Geneva, 1538

These prosperous beginnings did greatly mislike Satan and his, who failed not (as it was an easy matter to do in the first change of the estate of Religion) to set himself against the proceeding of the Gospel.... Master Calvin ... withstood firmly and constantly with Master Farel the seditious persons ... it was ordained (the greater part of the Council not being the best) that the forenamed should depart the town within twenty-four hours, because they would not minister the Supper of the Lord in a city that was so troubled and stirred. When this was declared to the said Calvin, his answer was that if he had served men, he should have been ill recompensed, but he served Him, who instead of evil recompensing his servants, did always give them more than they deserved. And he might justly so say: for he had followed the example of St Paul, in serving of the Church upon his own charge and cost.

From Theodore Beza: *Life of Calvin* (1564)

C Calvin's pattern of Church leadership
First there are four orders of offices instituted by our Saviour for the government of his Church: namely, the pastors, then the doctors, next the elders (nominated and appointed by the government), and fourthly the deacons. If we wish to see the Church well-ordered and maintained we ought to observe this form of government.

The duty of pastors
Pastors are sometimes named in the Bible as overseers, elders and ministers. Their work is to proclaim the Word of God, to teach, admonish, exhort and reprove publicly and privately, to administer the sacraments and, with the elders or their deputies, to issue fraternal warnings .....

There follows the second order which we have called the doctors
The special duty of the doctors is to instruct the faithful in sound doctrine so that the purity of the gospel is not corrupted by ignorance or wrong opinion.

As things stand at present, every agent assisting in the upholding of God's teaching is included so that the Church is not in difficulties from a lack of pastors and ministers. This is in common parlance the order of school teachers. The degree nearest the minister and closely joined to the government of the Church is the lecturer in theology ...

Here follows the third order, or elders
Their duty is to supervise every person's conduct. In friendly fashion they should warn backsliders and those of disorderly life. After that, where necessary, they should report to the Company (or pastors) who will arrange for fraternal correction ...

As our Church is now arranged, it would be most suitable to have two elected from the 'council of 24', four from the 'council of 60' and six from the 'council of 200'. They should be men of good repute and conduct ... They should be chosen from each quarter of the city so that they can keep an eye on the whole of it ...

The fourth order of ecclesiastical government, namely, the deacons
There have always been two kinds of these in the early Church. One has to receive, distribute and care for the goods of the poor (i.e. daily alms as well as possessions, rents and pensions); the other has to tend and look after the sick and administer the allowances to the poor as is customary.

From Jean Calvin: *The Ecclesiastical Ordinances of Geneva* (1541)

D   Calvin's Dealings with his Religious Opponents in Geneva
And another time, to wit the year of our Lord 1553 Michel Servet a Spaniard of cursed memory, happened to come, who was not a man, but rather, an horrible Monster, compounded of the ancient and new heresies, and above all an execrable blasphemer against the Trinity, and namely against the Eternity of the Son of God.

About two years before there came a certain deceitful Friar, a Carmelite, suddenly become a divine, a Physician, named Hierosme Bolsec of Paris, who ... began in open congregation to condemn the doctrine of the eternal providence and predestination, as though we made God the author of sin, and culpable in the condemnation of the wicked: Calvin ... did so answer him by word both openly and privately, and afterward also by writing that the adversary had no truth of his side remaining, but a certain Monkish shamelessness which made him and doth make him at this daye filthy and stinking to every man that hath any good understanding.

I have also omitted one Monster which he likewise did defeat, albeit that in that behalf I fought on his side: it is one named Sebastian Castellio, who because he had some knowledge in the tongues, and had also a certain aptness in the Latin tongue, he was here received to govern the school. But this spirit being so naturally inclined to please himself, did so dive him in his vanity that in the end he drowned himself therein, because we could never win so much of him, as to cause him to take the pains to read the Commentaries and other works to resolve him. That was the cause why he did openly condemn the song called Canticum Canticorum, in Latin, as a filthy and wanton Book: which when it was laid to his charge, he vomited out openly a thousand injuries against the pastors of this Church: whereupon being commanded by the Magistrate to avouch his sayings, and being of manifest malice and evil speaking, by justice he was appointed to depart the town after he had acknowledged his fault: being in the end retired to Basle.

From Theodore Beza: *Life of Calvin* (1564)

E The Political Opposition of the Libertines

After your departure the dances caused us more trouble than I had supposed. All those who were present being summoned to the Consistory, with the two exceptions of Corne and Perrin, shamelessly lied to God and us. I was incensed, as the vileness of the thing demanded, and I strongly inveighed against the contempt of God in that they thought nothing of making a mockery of the sacred obtestations we had used. They persisted in their contumacy. When I was fully informed of the state of the case, I could do nothing but call God to witness that they would pay the penalty of such perfidy; I, at the same time however, announced my resolution of revealing the truth, even though it should be at the cost of my own life, lest they should imagine that any profit was to come of lying. Francisca also, the wife of Perrin, grossly abused us, because we were so opposed to the Favres. I replied as seemed proper, and as she deserved. I inquired whether their house was inviolably sacred, whether it owed no subjection to the laws? We already detained her father in prison, being convicted of one act of adultery, the proof of a second was close at hand; there was a strong report of a third; her brother had openly contemned and derided the Senate and us. Finally I added that a new city must be built for them, in which they might live apart, unless they were willing to be restrained by us here under the yoke of Christ; that so long as they were in Geneva, they would strive in vain to cast off obedience to the laws; for were there as many diadems in the house of Favre as frenzied heads, that would be no barrier to the Lord being superior. Her husband meanwhile had gone to Lyons, hoping that the matter would be silently buried. I thought that they should be forced to a confession of the truth by an oath. Corne warned them that he would by no means suffer them to perjure themselves. They not only confessed what we wished, but that they on that day danced at the house of the widow of Balthazar. They were all cast into prison. The Syndic was an illustrious example of moderation; for he publicly spoke against himself and the whole herd so severely that it was unnecessary to say much to him. He was, however, severely admonished in the Consistory, being deposed from his office until he gave proof of repentance. They say that Perrin has returned from Lyons; whatever he may do he will not escape punishment.

From a letter from Calvin to Farel, April 1546

F Changes in the Consistory

Thursday 1 February. Assent is here given to the proposition and request recently made by the ministers touching the reformation of the Consistory and of ecclesiastical jurisdiction.

On the first point of their request, namely that in elections to the Consistory one should have liberty to elect anyone who is a member of the Council of Two Hundred, without distinction between citizens and burgesses: for when one is endeavouring to follow the Word of God one needs freedom to choose the most suitable candidates from among the entire people.

It was decided also that such a reading also demands that the elders be selected from the entire Council of Two Hundred without distinction between citizens and burgesses, although this is not specifically contained in the Edicts.

For that matter is was also requested that it be laid down that the Lord Syndic's role in the Consistory shall be such that the temporal jurisdiction is kept quite separate from the spiritual: for the Edicts do not state that he should preside or possess any jurisdiction there; the practice should be that a Syndic who is present will not carry his staff of office, but shall merely take his place there among the other elders.

From an edict reforming the Consistory, 1560

Questions

1 According to Source A, why was Calvin reluctant to remain in Geneva when he first arrived there?   **(4 marks)**

2 From Source C and your own knowledge explain why the fourfold ministry became such an important model outside of Geneva.

(8 marks)

3 Comment on the reliability of Beza's remarks on Calvin's opponents in Source D?   **(6 marks)**

4 Compare Sources D and E. Which opposition do you consider posed the more serious threat to Calvin's position in Geneva?   **(7 marks)**

5 What light do Sources A - F shed on the changing nature of Calvin's position in Geneva from 1536 - 64?   **(10 marks)**

13 CALVIN THE POLITICAL THINKER

The spread of his influence beyond Geneva presented Calvin with particular difficulties. As he attracted followers in his native France and also in the Netherlands, Calvin was forced to make spiritual judgements with political consequences. Luther (see Chapter 8) had been extremely reluctant to sanction conventicles. Calvin, similarly, was singularly unhelpful to his followers in the 1540s. Whilst he did not forbid their meeting in conventicle, he roundly condemned 'Nicodemism', the practice of holding Protestant beliefs privately, while publicly adhering to Catholicism. He offered only two rather stark alternatives - martyrdom or exile. By 1554, however, he was becoming more energetic and practical in his assistance, giving his advice on how congregations ought to organise themselves with a Consistory to bring discipline and a minister to preach and administer the sacraments.

In giving such advice Calvin was, of course, opposing the expressed wishes of the French king, Henry II. Calvin was unwilling to do this for two reasons. In the first place, he had long hoped for a reform of the entire French Church and separate organisation was, in some senses, therefore an admission of defeat. Second, resistance (as for any Protestant Bible-believing theologian), presented theological problems for Calvin. St. Paul in Romans 13 teaches that since all authority is ordained by God, Christians have a duty to submit even to tyrannical rulers. Calvin was therefore anxious to emphasise that he favoured only *passive* resistance, that is, disobedience to the law which stopped short of Reformed Protestants taking up arms.

Towards the end of his life, however, as the strength of Reformed Protestantism grew in France, Calvin was in no position to control events. Geneva sent 88 ministers across the border between 1555 and 1562 but, by the outbreak of the Wars of Religion, there were perhaps as many as 1,750 Reformed congregations in France. French Calvinism was fast becoming more militant than Calvin himself. Iconoclasm, psalm-singing demonstrations and plots against the Catholic Guise faction who controlled the teenage King Francis II after the sudden death of his father Henry II, all went further than Calvin would have liked. How did Calvin deal with this? To what extent was Calvin indebted to Lutheran arguments developed in 1530-31 with the formation of the Schmalkaldic League in his legitimising of armed resistance? Was his assertion that God appointed lesser magistrates (nobles) to oppose tyrannical rulers merely an argument of convenience? It should be considered whether resistance would have been possible without the leadership of Calvinist princes of the blood, such as Antoine de Bourbon, King of Navarre, and his brother Louis, Prince of Conde.

A Henry Seeks to Prevent Calvin's Influence in France

XXI. And because various offences have been committed by pedlars who under colour of selling some other sort of merchandise carry secretly books coming from Geneva and other places of ill fame, from now on it will not be permitted to the said pedlars to sell books, large or small, but if any of them carry them or expose them for sale, the books shall be seized, remitted into our hand and confiscated by us together with all other merchandise which they are carrying. In addition they shall be punished for contravention of this present article according to their quality and as the judges see fit.

XXXVII. We expressly forbid all our said subjects to write, to send money or otherwise to favour those who have gone out of the kingdom to reside in Geneva or in other countries notoriously separated from the union of the Church and the obedience of the Apostolic Holy See, on pain of being declared favourers of heretics and as such disobedient persons, infractors and contravenors of the ordinances and edicts of ourselves and of the late King our father, to be punished exemplarily ...

XXXVIII. All carriers of letters coming from Geneva will be arrested and published if it is found that the said letters are directed towards the end of diverting our subjects away from the truth and the observation of our faith and religion and into disobedience to the constitutions of the Church and will be proceeded against as true heretics and disturbers of public repose and peace.

The Edict of Chateaubriand (1551)

B Calvin Advocates Secret Meetings of his Followers in France So As to Avoid Persecution

You must be resolved on following up the business and organisation of assembling yourselves which you have already begun. We do not require you to make a public confession of your faith, for we are well aware of the strict tutelage in which you are held, and under these circumstances it is quite sufficient that the little flock should assemble in secret. As a result, it is necessary that you should agree amongst yourselves to meet both for joint prayers and for the preaching of the Word, in order to have the form of the church. This established, when there is someone among you who is fit to be called to the office of pastor, it will be his duty to administer the sacraments to you. But take heed that those who came forward with you to receive the sacraments in such purity as God has ordained are not still contaminated with papal superstitions, but that you may, in reality, be separated from anything which is opposed to our Lord Jesus Christ.

From a letter from Calvin to a French congregation, June 1554

C   Calvin on Resistance to the Civil Authorities

We must be very careful not to despise or violate that authority of magistrates, full of venerable majesty, which God has established by the weightiest decrees, even though it may reside with their own wickedness. For, if the correction of unbridled despotism is the Lord's to avenge, let us not at once think that it is entrusted to us, to whom no command has been given except to obey and suffer.

I am speaking all the while of private individuals. For if there are now any magistrates of the people, appointed to restrain the wilfulness of kings (as in ancient times the ephors were set against the Spartan kings, or the tribunes of the people against the Roman consuls, or the demarchs against the senate of the Athenians; and perhaps, as things now are, such power as the three estates exercise in every realm when they hold their chief assemblies), I am so far from forbidding them to withstand, in accordance with their duty, the fierce licentiousness of kings, that, if they wink at kings who violently fall upon and assault the lowly common folk, I declare that their dissimulation involves nefarious perfidy, because they dishonestly betray the freedom of the people, of which they know that they have been appointed protectors of God's ordinance.

From Jean Calvin: *Institutes* (1559)

D   Calvinist Divisions Over the Conspiracy of Amboise

Between 1555 and 1562 there were many plots against the French government. Not all were planned by Calvinists, but all involved Geneva in some way. The best known is the Conspiracy of Amboise in March 1560. This was an attempt to seize the young king, Francis II, to get rid of his Guise ministers and put France under a Bourbon regent. The chief conspirator, La Renaudie, visited Geneva beforehand in the hope of winning the support of the Venerable Company. Calvin opposed the plot, if only because it was not led by Anthony of Bourbon, the only man in his view with any right to be regent. His opinion, however, was not shared by all the pastors. De Beze allegedly gave secret encouragement to La Renaudie. Most of the Calvinist churches, however, preferred to follow Calvin's lead, which goes far to explain why the plot failed so dismally.

From R.W. Knecht: *The French Wars of Religion 1559 - 1598* (1989)

E   Calvin is Consulted on the Proposed Conspiracy of Amboise

Calvin said that it was true that Chandieu [the minister of the Church in Paris] had come here and that they had talked together about the tyranny which prevails at the present time and about what could be done to remedy the situation. He had argued with him and had pointed out that for all kinds of reasons the enterprise, in the form in which it was being planned, was not based upon the Word of God. He had agreed, however, that the time had now come when one could say that it was necessary and one's duty, to do something, for the sake of justice and of the order established by the laws of France, but without the spilling of human blood ...

However, he did admit to having said something like this to Chandieu: that if some great man of the King's Council, someone who had the right to be at the head of the kingdom, in accordance with the laws of France, acknowledged this, and declared himself, and that if there was no question of proceeding in any way other than strictly according to the law, without violence or resort to arms, then it would be proper for such a man to take control, provided that all the Courts of Parlement, the nobility and the people were in favour of the cause. He admitted also that the aforesaid Chandieu argued with him, but that he would not go further, insisting that it was not licit to do so, according to the Word of God. And what is more, once a single drop of blood was spilt, the gutters would run red with it everywhere, and that nobody would be able to prevent the most horrible disorder, and that it would be better for us all to die than to bring the Gospel into such disrepute.

An examination of the Genevan ministers concerning a statement by Jean Morely, a French Calvinist nobleman, 1560

F Calvin's Relief at the Death of Francis II
Did you ever read or hear of anything more opportune than the death of the King? The evils had reached an extremity for which there was not remedy, when all of a sudden God shows himself from heaven. He who pierced the eye of the father has now struck the ear of the son. My only apprehension is lest some persons in the excess of their triumph defeat the hopes of an amelioration in our condition. For one can hardly believe how inconsiderately many people exult, nay wanton in their joy. They wish to transform the whole world in an instant, and because I do not countenance their folly they tax me with supineness. But to me it is enough that God approves of my diligence, and even more than enough to have in my favour the testimony of impartial and moderate men: these are not in a majority it is true, but I prefer their calm judgements to the noisy outcries of the multitude. They would wish me to act along with the King of Navaree in his turbulent projects, as if, indeed, supposing him to be the most sagacious and vigorous of mortals, it was in his power to grant what they so preposterously demand. I, on the contrary, am so opposed to

this precipitancy that it gave me no small accession of joy to learn that his brother was unwilling to quit his prison. I had already previously given my advice to such an effect, so that I rejoice that more heartily that what I deemed to most salutary proceeding has spontaneously suggested itself to their minds.

From a letter from Calvin to Johann Sturm, December 1560

Questions

1 Study Source A. Why was Calvinism seen as such a threat by the French monarch? **(4 marks)**

2 What, according to Source B, constituted a Calvinist Church? How was that Church to operate? **(6 marks)**

3 Compare and contract Sources C, D and E. How do they explain the extent and limitations of Calvin's views on resistance? **(10 marks)**

4 From Source F and your own knowledge explain why Calvin was so relieved at the death of Francis II. **(8 marks)**

5 To what extent do the Sources confirm the view that Calvinism was a revolutionary creed? **(12 marks)**

14 THE ROLE OF CALVINISM IN THE WARS OF RELIGION

It seemed in 1561-2, on the eve of the Wars of Religion, that Calvinism was capable of capturing and reforming the whole of France, such had been its meteoric growth over the previous seven years. The Reformed had held their first national synod in Paris in May 1559 at which they had created a Confession of Faith and a new pyramidal system of Church government, with provincial synods and colloquies acting as regional and local structures between the congregational and national synod levels. They had as many as 1,750 congregations numbering perhaps two million people, concentrated particularly from La Rochelle to Dauphiné across southern France, and had attracted especially strong support from artisans and the nobility.

It was the large numbers of noble converts - perhaps as many as 40 per cent of the entire French nobility - which ultimately drove Calvinism towards civil war. The French monarchy had been left in a particularly weak state in 1559 with the sudden death of Henry II, the throne passing to his 15 year old sickly son, Francis II. Although Francis was technically old enough to rule, real power passed to the Guise faction at court. The ascendancy of the fanatically Catholic Guise family caused resentments within the other two great noble families, the Montmorency and the Bourbon. It was not until the reign of Henry IV (1589-1610) that France again had a king strong enough to assert the authority of the French monarchy. Thus, the origins of the Wars of Religion do not lie solely with the growth of Calvinism. Religion provided the ideological cause for which people fought, but factional infighting produced by a power vacuum also played an important part.

How much did it benefit from the political protection it gained from its noble pedigree and how much did it suffer from its association in the minds of the French people with the shedding of blood? To what extent, and why, was it forced to become increasingly radical through civil war, particularly after the St. Bartholomew's Day Massacre?

A Calvin Predicts Violence in France
Meanwhile, everything is tending towards a horrible butchery because those who have professed themselves the disciples of Christ and have frequented secret assemblies [in] France are denounced as apostates.

From a letter from Calvin to an admirer, 4 October 1559

B The Growth of Calvinism

In many cities [in France] the papists have broken out in tumults, not without bloodshed. In Paris they have been twice vigorously repressed and severely manhandled. The court of parlement there not only deceives us, but seems to consider it an advantage to kindle animosity against us. Despite that, it is incredible how the kingdom of God is spreading far and wide. From all sides the demands for ministers are addressed to us, and though we have no more to send, yet such is their insistence that we have to choose certain ministers from the lower ranks of the people. The parlement of Toulouse is even more atrocious than that of Paris. Many are still in prison there.

From a letter from Calvin to Ambrose Blaurer, May 1561

C A Prediction of Civil War

Your Serenity will hardly believe the influence and the great power which the principal minister of Geneva, by name Calvin, a Frenchman, and a native of Picardy, possesses in this kingdom; he is a man of extraordinary authority, who by his mode of life, his doctrines, and his writings, rises superior to all the rest; and it is almost impossible to believe the enormous sums of money which are secretly sent to him from France to maintain his power. It is sufficient to add that if God does not interfere, there is great and imminent danger that one of two things will happen in this kingdom: either that the truce, which is desired and sought publicly, will end by the heretics having churches wherein they can preach, read, and perform their rites, according to their doctrine, without hindrance, and in like manner as they obtained churches by command of the late king, given at Fontainbleau, at the end of August, in compliance with a petition presented to him by the Admiral [Coligny]; or, else, that we shall see an obedience to the Pope and to the Catholic rites enforced, and shall have resort to violence and imbrue our hands in noble blood. For these reasons I foresee a manifest and certain division in the kingdom, and civil war as a consequence; and this will be the cause of the ruin both of the kingdom and of religion, because upon a change in religion a change in the State necessarily follows.

From the report of the Venetian ambassador in France, 1561

D Calvinist Churches in France in 1562

From A.E. McGrath: *A Life of John Calvin* (1990)

E The Militarisation of Calvinism

The first civil war had lasted less than a year but its legacy was militarised Calvinism and sectarian fury. The Conspiracy of Amboise had not received the backing of the churches, but now the synod of Clairac gave a paramilitary structure to the churches of Guyenne. The system was adopted in southern France and Condé's [Louis de Bourbon] title of Protector-General of the churches of France fitted the facts. When war came Beza acted as chaplain to the psalm-singing troops of Condé and orders were despatched by both to the churches for men and money. Political assemblies, adjuncts of the synods, came into existence to co-ordinate the war-effort. Antoine de Crussol was nominated as head of the Calvinist forces in Languedoc and Dauphine. Two subordinate councils issued in 1563 a detailed directive of 136 articles, which covered the enforcement of the Discipline, salaries of ministers, charity for the poor and for the war victims, inventories of church property and plate, a loan to be raised from nobles and wealthy citizens, and a scale of payment for troops, starting with 6,000 livres for Crussol.

From M. Prestwich: *International Calvinism 1541 - 1715* (1985)

F   The St. Bartholomew's Day Massacre, 24 August 1572
On the fourth day after the wedding celebrations of the King of Navarre, which passed off peacefully enough, the Lord Admiral (whom even his enemies admit to have been the wisest and most outstanding of men, on account of the integrity of his mind) was returning from the King's Court to his lodging, reading on the way certain letters that had been handed to him, when two bullets fired by a hired marksman from the window of a house wounded him in such a way that although his body was not injured, one of the bullets took away his right thumb and the other went right through his left arm.

During the evening of the 23rd it became clear that the wounds were not going to prove fatal, and it was after this that assassins were sent, before dawn on the 24th, from the town to the lodging of our people, an easy way for them to get in having been planned in advance. They cruelly hacked many to death as they slept, and then they all fell at once upon the Admiral, inflicting upon him so many wounds that he fell to the floor semi-conscious. As for the guards posted by the King, not only did they fail to resist, they made the assassination possible, and took a leading part in it, killing without exception all those who did not manage to escape, noblemen, domestics, and others. They hacked the Admiral, inflicting many wounds. Not content with this they threw his body out of the window for the crowd to tear apart. Then the whole town became a scene of Massacre. So great was the mad rage that no distinction was made of age, sex or condition. Navarre and Condé only just managed to escape, and there is a rumour, still unconfirmed, that they have been poisoned. Some of the assembled noblemen tried to put up a resistance but in the end a great many were killed, only a very few escaping by making their way into the suburbs and taking flight. It is reported that thirty-two noblemen of the first rank, the most pro-minent of the leaders of our party, as well as eighty gentlemen of lower rank lost their lives: simply because they attended the wedding festivities of the King of Navarre. And out of the rest of the popula-tion, if what is being said is true, no less than 8,000 were slain.

From a letter from Theodore Beza to a German Calvinist, 4 September 1572

G Resistance Theory
Thus, the law of nature, the law of peoples, and civil law command us to take arms against tyrants without title, nor is there any legal scruple to detain us - no oath or compact whatsoever, entered into either publicly or privately. Therefore, when this kind of tyranny occurs, anyone may act to drive it out, including private individuals ...

The obligation between prince and people is ever reciprocal and mutual. He promises to be a just prince; they, to obey him if he is one. The people, therefore, is obligated to the prince conditionally, he to the people absolutely. If the condition is not fulfilled, the people are released, the compact voided and the obligation nullified. The king is perjured if he rules unjustly; the people, if they fail to obey him when his rule is just. The people, however, is absolved from any charge of perjury if it publicly renounces a ruler who would rule unjustly or if it attempts, by force of arms, to evict a ruler who seeks to retain possession of the kingdom in contravention of the law.

From Philippe Duplessis Mornay: *Defence Against Tyrants* (1579)

Questions

1 Examine Sources C and D. What light do they shed on the causes of the outbreak of civil war in France in 1562?   **(4 marks)**

2 Compare Sources A and B with source C. How and why do they differ in their attribution of blame?   **(6 marks)**

3 How reliable is Source F as an account of the St. Bartholomew's Day Massacre?   **(7 marks)**

4 Compare Source G with Source C in Chapter 13. How is it possible to explain the differences between the two texts?   **(8 marks)**

5 To what extent do Sources A - G suggest that 'Wars of Religion' is an apt term to describe the conflicts in French society from 1562 - 98?   **(10 marks)**

15

THE ROLE OF CALVINISM
IN THE DUTCH REVOLT

The origins of the Dutch Revolt are extremely complex. As early as 1561 the absent Philip II was making himself unpopular through his centralising policies epitomised in Cardinal Granvelle's 'new bishoprics' scheme. There was dislike of what was perceived as a growing Spanish influence, seen both in the appointments of advisers to Margaret of Parma (Philip's regent in the Netherlands), and in the deployment of troops. The increasing number of Spanish officials particularly infuriated the Netherlandish nobility who felt their own position to be under threat. In addition, Philip's anti-heresy legislation was far from popular, particularly in the towns where the local magistrates resented the encroaching powers of central government and feared destruction of their traditional 'liberties'. By 1565 there was also a small number of Calvinist nobles prepared to push for an end to repression. The high nobility at this point - men such as Orange, Egmont and Hornes - remained Catholic, but found heresy trials distasteful. Faced with pressure from higher and lesser nobles alike, Margaret of Parma was vacillating and weak. The economic situation in 1565-6 was bleak. Bad weather ruined harvests and produced spiralling prices. In the midst of all this, Calvinism made increasingly strong headway.

Calvinism had first begun to make inroads into the southern, French-speaking Low Countries as early as 1543-4. Ten years later Calvin's writings began to appear in Dutch and, in 1555, a Calvinist church was established in Antwerp. Between 1555 and the early 1560s membership of the Reformed Church in the Netherlands remained numerically small. The costs of membership, in terms of the risks involved and the strict discipline imposed, were high, although the Calvinist churches in the southern Netherlands received an influx of members with the outbreak of the French Wars of Religion in 1562 because local magistrates were prepared to turn a blind eye to heresy. However, Calvinism's public emergence on a wide stage did not occur until the 'hedgepreaching' in the summer of 1566. The extent to which the Calvinists benefited from the collapse in the authority of Margaret of Parma's government and the extent to which their message was inherently appealing should be considered. Also there is the issue of the reasons for the iconoclastic riots. Were they spontaneous outbursts of popular anger at Catholic idolatry or were they, as some historians have suggested, organised by the Consistories and carried out for payment by the unemployed, by whores, drunkards and teenage boys? The importance of Calvinist preachers' railings against images as a catalyst sparking the Revolt should also be considered.

There are two strands which run throughout the Dutch Revolt down to the Twelve Years Truce of 1609. First, the towns of the Netherlands were prepared to go to considerable lengths to defend their 'liberties' against Spanish domination, hence the resentment at the introduction of the Duke of Alva's Tenth Penny tax in March 1569 (indeed the dislike of Alva's entire regime), and the coming together of the seventeen provinces in the Pacification of Ghent in 1576, brought about by the mutinies of Spanish troops. The second theme running through Dutch resistance is freedom of worship for the Calvinists. How important was toleration in prolonging the Revolt? To what extent did it act as a sticking point in peace negotiations between the Spanish and the rebels? It has been estimated that, during the Duke of Parma's reconquests in the 1580s, as many as 150,000 Calvinists emigrated north so that they could continue to practice their religion. Would it be true to say that all Parma's concessions in the south were of little consequence since Philip II refused to budge on the one issue of real import?

A Philip II Gives Advice on Religious Affairs
I cannot refrain from telling you that considering the condition of religious affairs in the Netherlands as I understand it, this is no time to make any alteration. On the contrary, His Majesty's edicts should be executed; I think that the cause of the past evil and its subsequent growth and advance has been the negligence leniency and duplicity of the judges, about which I will give you more particulars later. I told the prince of Gavre that since the men condemned to die advance to execution not in silence, but as martyrs dying for a cause you should consider whether they ought not to be executed in secret in some way or other (though it is true that a public execution also serves to set an example) ...

For the rest I can only thank you for all you propose to me, but assure you that my orders are designed for the welfare of religion and of my provinces and are worth nothing if they are not obeyed. In this way you can keep my provinces in justice, peace and tranquillity. Now that you know the importance of this, I pray you again to take steps to bring this state of affairs into being.

From a letter from Philip II to Margaret of Parma, 17 October 1565

B Hedgepreaching in Lille
... I am bound, furthermore, to inform Your Highness that two more preachings took place last night, the chief of which, attended by some 4,000 people, was held about two leagues from this town on the road to Tournai by a preacher whose name, I understand, is Cornille de La Zenne, the son of a blacksmith from Roubaix, who has long been a fugitive from this country on account of the religion. According to the

report, which some reliable persons have submitted to me, whom I know to have been at the said preaching, the said preacher exhorted his auditors, among other things, not to start any trouble or [commit] any seditious act, because in such a case no one would assist them, but if anyone arrested them or examined them for no other reason than their faith, or for having gone to the preachings, they might all be assured that they would be helped before any ill befell them, and in conclusion he spoke more or less as follows; we pray to God that He may grant the destruction of this papist idolatry; be of good heart for we are quite strong, but our time has not yet come. And we pray God that He may keep the people of Tournai and Armentieres in their convictions and likewise confirm the good start we see among the inhabitants of Lille. And when the said sermon was over, the preacher disappeared so quickly through the crowd with the help of twenty hackbutters, who escorted him, that it was impossible to know whither he had retired.

From a letter from the governor of Lille to Margaret of Parma, June 1566

C Iconoclasm in Antwerp, August 1566

The Virgin's image, that had been carried about in procession only two days before, was the first to suffer. The chapel in which it stood was entered by force, and the idol thrown down and dashed to pieces, all the people roaring, 'Vive les Gueux'. They then attacked the other statues, pictures and altars as well as the organ, heedless of their antiquity, beauty or value. They cast down or plundered these with such vehemence and headlong insolence that before midnight they had reduced one of the largest, most glorious and splendidly adorned churches in Europe with its seventy altars to an empty and ghastly hulk. No locks were strong enough to protect the treasures entrusted to them. Yet there was no quarrelling about the booty: indeed, no less strange, in the confused commotion of this raging mob, which perpetrated so many excesses, there was such unity and orderliness that it seemed as if each person had been allotted his task before-hand. Remarkably, while they vied with one another to climb the ladders, laboured to cast down the great marble-stones and heavy pieces of copper, and eagerly plundered the choicest pieces, not one out of this entire multitude hurt himself by falling and no one was injured in the slightest by the descent of objects as they crashed down and fragments flew in all directions, or by colliding and knocking into those who, wielding their instruments of destruction, pressed on to break everything. In the eyes of some this appeared so strange that they attributed a role to the hellish spirits in this transaction, scarcely believing that it could be the work of men. When they had finished in the principal church, they fan through the streets, carrying lighted candles and stolen tapers, like men possessed and escaped lunatics, roaring 'Vive les Gueux' and demolishing all the crosses and images in sight. Driven on by the same fury, and reinforced by fresh numbers, they flew to other churches, chapels and monasteries, where they not only mishandled stocks and stones, but living creatures too, among whom the Franciscans fared the worst. They broke open chambers and cellars; stove in all the barrels, and set the floor awash with beer and wine.

From G. Brandt: *The History of the Reformation in the Low Countries* (1671)

D Responsibility for the Iconoclasm at Antwerp

Herman Modet, one of the most zealous preachers ... declares in a certain apology which he published soon after these disorders that neither he himself nor any of his Consistory had any more knowledge of the plan to destroy images when it was first conceived than at the hour of their death ...

... As he returned to his lodging in the evening, he was informed that the Church was full of people, and he had hardly come into his house before he heard that they had attacked the images. The objection was made that he was in the Church whilst they were breaking and defacing them. This he admitted was true but added that this was the desire of the magistrates themselves, and it was at the peril of his own life that he went in to quieten the mob. As he did so he was pulled down from the pulpit and thrown out of the Church. He returned there about five hours later having been asked to do so, in order to warn the people not to plunder and steal under the pretence of demolishing idols.

From G. Brandt: *The History of the Reformation in the Low Countries* (1671)

E A Calvinist's View of Responsibility for the Iconoclasm

I concede that among the image breakers there were people who professed to be of the religion, but I also say that there were as many others who did not make and never made that profession. In several places one even saw only women and children busily destroying things. In several other places the bishops and priests began to hide their most beautiful rings and the citizens followed suit, thinking that orders had been given to hide whatever might be saved, until the children and street-boys destroyed the rest. In some places the magistrates sent their officers to accomplish the task and they were followed by the common people. Even now one does not know who were the originators. There are, however, strong suspicions and clear indications that it was the priests who started this as a device to set the magistrates against those of the religion (in the past they undoubtedly often did such things to cause new persecutions), as well as to ruin the plan, unanimously accepted by all the churches to send a request to Her Highness. Time was short for the priests and their adherents realised that if the churches' plea were indeed accomplished, their own little schemes would be entirely wrecked. And indeed, after the troubles at Antwerp had died down another riot was instigated by some who forced their way into the Church of Our Lady. Six of those responsible were apprehended and hanged the day after. There were four papists among them and one of these was a well-known nobleman who had urged the others on. So we have to presume that by means of such a stratagem they tried to wreck the churches' plan. This is proved by later events for, because of this, the request was not presented and those of the religion afterwards met with nothing but disfavour and hatred.

From a pamphlet by Philip Marnix, a leading Dutch Calvinist, written in 1567

F A Controversy at Leiden, 1574
Those on the side of the States remained steadfast in their aim of asserting the liberties of their country to the uttermost, especially at Leiden where, during the siege, they issued paper currency of 14 and 28 stuivers value, because of a lack of silver. The 14 stuiver note was stamped on one side with a lion holding a sword and a shield with the motto 'I fight for my country'. The 28 stuiver note had lion, holding a hat on a spear with the motto 'All this for liberty', meaning that they had acted and suffered for the cause of liberty. But the Calvinist preachers did not hesitate to attack their rulers from the pulpit, calling them libertines and free thinkers, arguing that they ought to have said 'This is for religion', as if freedom of religion was not part of the general expression of liberty, and as if others out of horror for the Inquisition and Spanish government had not fought bravely for their country, even though they were not Protestants.

From G. Brandt: *The History of the Reformation in the Low Countries* (1671)

G The Peace Negotiations at Breda, 1575
His princely Highness [Orange] and the States have always declared openly that their intention was by no means to arm themselves against His Majesty or to desert him or to be alienated or separated from him, but to keep themselves united with other countries under His Majesty. Nor was it ever their intention to take or withhold or seize goods from spiritual or temporal persons who did not assist their adversaries. Thus His Highness and the States cannot think that any good will come from what is now being proposed. They are particularly distressed by a number of conditions put by the other party which stipulate that the Roman Catholic religion should be

observed, that people should live according to the Roman Catholic rules or depart from the country etc. These suggest that the present religion is a heresy and those who observe it heretics. In reality, however, no other religion is being observed here than the catholic and apostolic religion, corresponding to the Holy Gospel and God's teaching, in which every one finds comfort and security. It is only the grave glaring abuses especially disagreeable to God Almighty that have been eliminated in order to render unto Caesar the things which are Caesar's and unto God the things which are God's.

From a contemporary pamphlet

H   The Peace Negotiations at Cologne, 1579
We know, following the great affection the King shows himself to have for his Roman religion, that by its rules he is under an obligation to make war with his subjects who do not want to follow this religion. For it is been resolved that he cannot grant liberty in his countries for the practice of any other than the Roman religion, and that having given himself to such unjust and tyrannical things as the laws of this Roman religion, he will not want to act against his conscience in order to accommodate his subjects, to whom until this hour he has shown so little affection. In addition to this the general and continual alliances he has with the pope, especially against the Reformed religion, whose adherents are considered by them as worse than the Turks and other enemies of the Christian name, do not permit him to reconcile himself with his subjects of any other religion but the Roman; to such an extent that he is pushed by his supposed religion to satisfy his supposed conscience, to continue the war against us or to trap us by a feigned peace.

From a contemporary pamphlet

Questions

1 How does Philip view the possibility of religious toleration in Source A? **(3 marks)**

2 From your own knowledge explain why, by 1566, the Calvinist preachers attracted the widespread support described in Source B. **(6 marks)**

3 Compare Source C with sources D and E. In the light of these Sources how responsible for the iconoclasm do you consider the Calvinists to be? **(8 marks)**

4 What evidence of bias can you detect in Source F? **(6 marks)**

5 Consider Sources A - H. How significant was religion in causing and continuing the Dutch Revolt 1566 - 79? **(12 marks)**

16 DEALING WITH EXAMINATION QUESTIONS

Specimen Source-based Question Answers (see Chapter 9, page 60)

1 What arguments are used by Hoen in Source A to oppose the real presence? **(4 marks)**

Hoen compares the bread and wine of communion to a wedding ring which symbolises the givenness of Christ to the believer, just as the ring represents the love of the groom for the bride. He further suggests that the adoration of the host as God is nothing short of idolatry, referring to Jesus' warnings in the Gospels that his followers should not believe anyone who claims to have found the Christ.

2 Compare and contrast Zwingli's and Luther's views of the Eucharist in Sources B and C. **(7 marks)**

Luther asserts the doctrine of the real presence in Source C whereas Zwingli repudiates it in Source B. The grounds of both men's defence of their views lie in Scripture. For Luther, Christ's words at the Last Supper as recorded in the Gospels are, he argues, to be taken literally and at face value. Thus, the body and blood of Christ are 'truly present' in the bread and wine respectively. For Zwingli, on the other hand, Christ's words cannot be understood literally. It is wrong, he claims, to base a whole doctrine on one text (as Luther has done), because one passage of Scripture needs to be compared with another. In addition, Zwingli uses two other arguments to refute the real presence. First, that it reduces Christians to nothing more than cannibals and second, that it contradicts the Creed. If Christ is at the right hand of God, Zwingli asserts, He cannot be also in the bread and wine of holy communion.

3 Comment on the purpose and tone of Source C **(6 marks)**

Published in 1526 , Source C is a direct attack by Luther on those who reject the real presence and is highly polemical in tone. This is seen clearly in the title of the pamphlet in which the real presence is asserted and anyone who chooses to believe otherwise is denounced as a fanatic (the German word is *Schwarmgeister*). This tract formed part of a literary dialogue, a war of words between Luther and Zwingli. Luther ridicules those who deny the real presence as hopelessly divided amongst themselves and, in Carlstadt's case, as adopting a ludicrous and nonsensical interpretation of Scripture. If those who reject the real presence cannot agree amongst themselves, Luther infers, how can their beliefs hold any

credence? For Luther, Zwingli is already discredited because of the
similarity of his views with those of Carlstadt who Luther had already
denounced as a 'fanatic' in 1522.

4   From Source D and your own knowledge explain the points of agreement
    and the points at issue at the Colloquy of Marburg.   **(6 marks)**

As can be seen from Source D, the Lord's Supper was the key point at issue
at Marburg. Although there were aspects of the Eucharist on which both
sides agreed - Luther and Zwingli alike rejected the Mass as a good work
and a sacrifice and believed that communion should be in two kinds - there
was deadlock on the real presence. Luther, supported by Melanchthon,
Brenz and Osiander, rejected the mere 'logic' and 'natural reason' of
Zwingli, Oecolampadius and Bucer. In addition, he refuted the Swiss claim
that, since Christ was seated at the right hand of the Father, He could not
also be in the bread, preferring the doctrine of the 'ubiquity' of Christ's
body. The closest the two sides reached was Zwingli's willingness to accept
the notion that Christ was present in the heart of the believer. The colloquy
concluded with an agreement on 14 of 15 articles. On the central doctrines
of the Christian faith - the Trinity, original sin, justification and the like -
there was no division, but this could not hide the failure of Philip of Hesse's
initiative.

5   Look at Sources A-F. How significant was the eucharistic controversy in
    limiting the success of the Reformation?   **(12 marks)**

Philip of Hesse called the Colloquy of Marburg because he hoped that a
theological agreement between the Lutherans and the Swiss would pave the
way to a military alliance against Charles V who posed an increasingly
serious threat to the Protestant cause. Charles, by 1529, had solved his
conflicts with Francis I of France and Pope Clement VII and thus was more
likely to gain the support of the Catholic princes in his declared intention
of suppressing Protestantism (Source E). In fact, there was little or no real
chance of a consensus view, since both camps had taken up sharply
contrasting views in the years before the colloquy (B and C) and Luther was
particularly polemical in tone (C). No agreement was forthcoming and this
had serious political and religious consequences. The lack of evangelical
unity meant that 'the political credibility of the Reformation was seriously
compromised' and Charles V was in a position to begin to reassert his
authority in the Empire (E). The Reformation was weakened also in
religious terms because an important Protestant principle, that of the clarity
of Scripture, had been weakened. The Reformation had set great store by
the Bible as the Word of God but it was now evident that it was possible to
interpret Scripture in radically different ways (E). Yet there was a degree of
unity amongst evangelicals in the post-Marburg period. For political reasons
German reformed cities such as Strasbourg moved away from Zwinglianism

towards Lutheranism in the hope of gaining the security that membership of the Schmalkaldic League brought. By the 1540s and '50s Calvin, ecumenical in his approach, taught a spiritual presence of Christ at the Lord's Supper which, although it failed to bring complete unity, did, to some extent, act as a healing balm (F).

Approaching Essays Questions

The key to writing successful history essays must always be in the last resort the ability to achieve relevance, in other words, you must answer the particular question set. Relevance is worth much more than length or a mass of detail. Accurate knowledge is also important, but only if it is employed to back up a particular argument, not for its own sake. Unanalytical narrative, or prepared answers to a topic which do not meet the requirements of the particular title set, are probably the commonest failings of examination answers. Conversely, the best answers are often concise, always relevant, analytical, and show evidence of wide and thoughtful reading. Your command of the English language is not being tested as such, but you must be able to present your arguments effectively.

Plan your essays. Break the question down into its key components. What are the key phrases or words in the question? Give your essays a shape: an introduction which will introduce the main argument and possibly indicate how you hope to approach it; a logical main body, written in paragraphs (sometimes ignored by students); and a conclusion which does not repeat the bulk of your essay but neatly draws together the threads. Other issues such as style and use of quotations are also important if you wish to write lucidly and well. As with most things in life, essay writing usually improves with practice.

In most of the history essays you encounter, you will be asked to evaluate a statement or quotation, or answer a direct question. There are usually different approaches you may adopt: therefore, 'model' answers must be treated with caution. It is, for example, quite in order to approach a controversial issue by considering evidence which supports different sides of an argument, without necessarily coming down decisively on one side of a particular interpretation. On the other hand, it is equally acceptable to argue a particular viewpoint, provided you can produce supporting evidence. Credit will usually be given if you show relevant knowledge of contemporary and/or more recent sources.

There are books available which deal in some depth with issues such as analytical reading, question analysis and essay-writing. Students may well find any of the following useful:

C. Brasher: *The Young Historian* (OUP, 1970)

J. Cloak, V. Crinnon and S. Harrison: *The Modern History Manual* (Framework Press, 1987)

J. Fines: *Studying to Succeed - History at 'A' Level and Beyond* (Longman, 1986)

The following list of essay titles on the Reformation includes suggestions (no more than suggestions) on how to approach them; plus a specimen answer. Use them as part of your course or for examination practice.

Possible Essay Titles

1 Why were the Pope and the Emperor so alarmed by Luther's teachings?

This essay requires you to focus on the period 1517-21 which saw Luther excommunicated and placed under imperial ban. Why did a fairly modest questioning, such as the Ninety Five Theses, inflame opinion so quickly? A good answer would identify particular views such as those on the sacraments which appeared to undermine the very basis of medieval Catholicism and thus inflamed papal opinion. You would also be expected to distinguish between papal and imperial alarm. Charles V opposed Luther as a loyal son of the Church but also because he wished to maintain the political unity of the Empire. Finally, you might consider both papal and imperial alarm in the light of the popular impact of Luther's ideas.

2 Why did Luther's teachings have such an impact on German society?

This question asks you to identify those factors which help explain the popularity of Luther's ideas. You would be expected to discuss the strength of anti-papal and anti-clerical sentiments in Germany on the eve of the Reformation. In his *Address to the Christian Nobility of the German Nation* Luther struck a nationalistic patriotic chord, invoking conciliatory anti-papal arguments. Other factors worthy of consideration might include the dissemination of Luther's ideas through the printing press and the impact of Christian humanism in helping to prepare the ground for Luther.

3 Was Lutheranism a princely or a popular Reformation?

The best approach to this question would be to establish evidence for both an official princely Reformation and a spontaneous popular movement. In support of a princely Reformation you might discuss Luther's dependence on Duke Frederick of Saxony, the conversion of princes to the Lutheran cause in the 1520s and '30s and the characteristics of the official Reformation such as the Lutheran catechism. In defence of a popular reform movement one could cite 50 or so imperial cities which went over to the Reformation and discuss specific cases to demonstrate the influence of popular pressure.

4 Why did Lutheranism attract support from German princes?

You would be expected to identify a variety of motives amongst a number of princes to score well on this question. Besides the personal motives of Duke Frederick of Saxony (never actually a Lutheran) who protected Luther out of pride for his recently created University of Wittenberg, one might distinguish between religious, political and economic factors. Some became deeply attached to the Lutheran creed, others saw an opportunity to gain control of the Church, to oppose Habsburg imperial power or to seize Church lands.

5 Why was Lutheranism so successful in Germany and so much less successful elsewhere?

This question falls neatly into two sections. In the first half you need to explain the particular circumstances which helped to establish Lutheranism in the Empire (see Question 2) and the political advantages to the German princes of conversion to the Reformation. In the second half of the essay the failure of Lutheranism elsewhere needs to be addressed. You should qualify this failure. Lutheranism *was* successful where it had princely support (e. g. Scandinavia) but, because of Luther's resistance to sanction resistance or conventiles (underground churches) no Lutheran churches were established in the Netherlands or France where the rulers were Catholic, even though Luther's ideas circulated quite widely. By the mid sixteenth century the Lutherans were turning in on themselves with theological disputes and Calvinism, with its better organisation and more thorough-going reform, was more attractive.

6 How far was Lutheranism a revolutionary creed?

This question can and should be interpreted on two different levels. First, how revolutionary were Luther's religious ideas? It can be argued that Luther, initially moderate, was driven to a more radical position as a result of the ferocity of the condemnation of him by his opponents. In 1517 he was not consciously embarking on a reformation of the Church. By 1520 certain ideas, especially his revision of sacramental theology might be deemed revolutionary. Politically, Luther was not at all revolutionary. He was fierce in his condemnation of the Peasants' War because of the misinterpretation of his ideas on Christian freedom and he was very reluctant to sanction even princely resistance to the Emperor up to 1530.

7 'The German Reformation was essentially about faith' - Discuss

This question requires discussion of the key aspects of the Lutheran creed - justification by faith alone, the priesthood of all believers, Christian freedom, the authority of Scripture and sacramental theology. A good answer would also seek to examine the impact of the Reformation at large - the practical reform of the Church, the destruction of monasticism, clerical marriage, changes in education and the like.

8 Why was Lutheranism adopted so readily in some parts of Germany but not
   in others by 1555?

   The views and motives of particular German princes are clearly central here
   (see Question 4), but a good answer will also contrast the urban success of
   the Reformation with its failure in the countryside and perhaps also point
   to particular urban failures.

9 To what extent did Erasmus and Luther differ as religious reformers?

   The key words in this question are 'To what extent'? Some attempt to
   identify similarities should be made: e.g. attacks on abuses, dislike of
   scholastic theology, admiration of Scripture and the Church Fathers.
   Differences should also be established. These are likely to include the
   reasons behind their superficial agreement on issues such as the importance of Scripture, their contrasting theocentric and mancentred
   perspectives and their diverging views on human nature culminating in
   their controversy over the Freedom of the Will in 1525.

10 Compare Luther and Zwingli as religious reformers

   Any answer to this question will identify the fundamental division between
   the two men over the nature of Christ's presence in the Eucharist. Time
   should also be spent in consideration of their contrasting backgrounds and
   theological training and the impact this had in shaping their thought, and
   on their differing views of the relationship between Church and State.

11 What was distinctive about the religious thought of Calvin?

   A good answer to this question will do more than focus on the obvious issue
   of predestination and election. Calvin's views on Scripture, justification and
   sanctification, the Eucharist and the organisation of the Church should be
   considered and contrasted with those of other reformers.

12 Why was Calvinism a revolutionary force?

   You are required for this question to explain the circumstances behind the
   revolutionary politics of Calvinism. Political radicalism was not created in a
   vacuum but in the context of expansion and persecution of Calvinist
   churches in the Netherlands and, in particular, in France. Some discussion
   of the increasingly revolutionary nature of Calvinism would be helpful.

13 Was Calvinism a revolutionary creed?

   This answer is likely to be a qualified yes. Its focus should be a contrast
   between Calvin's initial reluctance to sanction resistance and the limited
   circumstances in which he eventually permitted it on the one hand and, on
   the other hand, the insistence of his followers by the 1570s that resistance
   was not merely a right but a duty.

14 To what extent was Calvinism 'a faith for town-dwellers'?

This is a difficult question. At a superficial level it can be answered by a discussion of the impact of Reformed Protestantism in Geneva. A better response, however, would offer contrasts between Geneva, France, the Netherlands and Germany, discussing its urban impact and its level of success in the countryside of the United Provinces and in the territories of those princes who went over to the 'Second Reformation'.

Specimen Essay Answer

The essay below is not a model answer, nor does it represent the only approach. Nevertheless, it is a response which focuses on the question and is the type of answer which may be written under examination conditions, in about 45 minutes.

'Why did Calvinism spread so widely in the sixteenth century?'

Calvinism began as a missionary movement. Operating from Geneva, in exile for most of his ministry, Calvin always kept half an eye on developments in France and from 1554 onwards, was actively encouraging the organisation of underground churches in his native land. By the end of the sixteenth century, the movement Calvin had spawned exercised a significant influence also in the Netherlands, Germany, Hungary, Poland, England and Scotland. It seemed as if Calvin had produced a new kind of man, one who possessed a moral integrity, a sense of vocation, a capacity to organise and a faith rooted in the Old Testament and the grandeur of God. Yet, as Menna Prestwich has recently pointed out, Calvinism was never merely a faith for individuals. It had within it a sense, a clear sense, of its corporate responsibilities. At the height of the French Wars of Religion a Scottish Presbyterian, after receiving a letter from the Calvinist fortress of La Rochelle, wrote to a correspondent in London that it was 'no small comfort .... to brethren of one nation to understand the state of the brethren in others nations'. Thus, Calvin can be considered to have given birth to a genuinely international movement.

In some respects, the growth of Calvinism is linked to the stagnation of Lutheranism. Luther had conspicuously failed to provide the structures necessary for his followers to survive and organise in places like the Netherlands and France, where the prince was unsympathetic to the Reformation cause. By the 1530s the Lutherans were also turning in on themselves and becoming embroiled in theological controversies. From 1536 onwards, Luther was in dispute with his former disciple Johann Agricola and, with Luther's death in 1546, there came further division between the Philippists, followers of Melanchthon, and the strict Lutherans, supporters of Flacius Illyricus. Most importantly, Lutheranism had failed to produce what it had seemed to promise, a thorough-going reform of the Church in Germany. Lutheran theologians themselves had become disillusioned from 1530 to 1560 at their failure to improve religious practice and understanding. The Second (i.e. Calvinist) Reformation in Germany, which began in the 1560s, brought genuine reform to the Church, schools and universities and even to the State, along biblical lines. For princes such as the Elector Frederick III of the Palatinate, the first Calvinist prince in Germany, Reformed Protestantism succeeded where Lutheranism had failed.

Calvinism's international success cannot be divorced from the person of Calvin. He was a man both of ideological conviction and considerable organising abilities. In the *Institutes* (first edition 1536, final version 1559), Calvin produced *the* definitive statement of Protestant faith. Arranged in four books dealing with God the Father, Christ, the Holy Spirit and the Church and the Sacraments, it became a manual for would-be Reformed theologians and ministers. It had a logic and a systematic approach to rival the great medieval scholastic works of men such as Peter Lombard, which Protestantism, in its earliest years, had conspicuously lacked.

In his structuring of the Church in Geneva, also, Calvin provided a model for others to follow. On returning from his enforced exile in Strasbourg, Calvin published his *Ecclesiastical Ordinances* in November 1541 which provided his blueprint for Church government. Borrowing from Bucer, Calvin advocated a fourfold ministry, that of pastors, doctors, elders and deacons. The most important ministries were those of the pastors and elders who together made up the Consistory, a vital organ of government in Calvin's Church. The Consistory was responsible for the maintenance of discipline and the punishment of sin, which was of crucial importance to Calvin since he believed that it was vital to partake of the Lord's Supper in a worthy manner.

The beauty of the Consistory lay in its adaptability. In Geneva, the magistrates initially exercised dominance since, in its original form, the Consistory comprised nine pastors and twelve elders who had to be magistrates. This meant that the Consistory could be a tool in the hands of the secular authorities for the control of public morals. This did not escape the notice of the German princes. It was Frederick IV's declared intention to make the Palatinate 'a holy city, blessed and honoured by God'. By the end of his ministry, after a long struggle, Calvin had wrestled control of discipline away from the Genevan magistrates. Shortly before his death, the number of pastors was increased from nine to nineteen, thus giving them a majority over the elders. The power to discipline was therefore placed into the hands of the Church. Again, this was understood and appreciated abroad. In countries such as the Netherlands and France, where the Calvinists remained persecuted, the Consistory could be adapted so that it could function without the support of the civil authorities. Both pastors and elders could be appointed from within the Church and thus the Calvinists were able to operate with complete autonomy. Moreover, they were themselves able to create new structures such as national and provincial synods and colloquies.

Calvinism retained, throughout the sixteenth century, a belief in the rightness of its cause. It was able to exploit power vacuums such as existed in France after the death of Henry II in 1559 or the Netherlands during the rule of Margaret of Parma in 1565-6, for this very reason. In its earliest years when it was vigorously persecuted, devotees received encouragement from the martyrologies of Jean Crespin (1554) and Adriaen van Halmstede (1559). These encouraged Calvinists to link contemporary sufferings with those of the early Church and reinforced their conviction that 'God was on their side' and that, ultimately, good would triumph over evil. They took similar consolation from the doctrine of predestination. Far too much has been made of this teaching as an element of Calvin's personal theology. Its real significance was in providing an assurance, in the dark days of the French Wars of Religion and the Dutch Revolt, that the cause was worth fighting for. Calvinism spread so widely in the sixteenth century because its ultimate triumph was assured. The Calvinists really were the chosen people of God.

BIBLIOGRAPHY

There are extensive bibliographies on the Protestant Reformation in many specialist books. The titles listed are all useful and easily accessible.

R.H. Bainton: *Here I Stand* (Lion publishing, 1994) This is an old but eminently readable biography of Luther which focuses particularly on his early life.

E. Cameron: *The European Reformation* (Clarendon Press, 1991) This is easily the best scholarly survey of the whole subject.

A.C. Duke: *Reformation and Revolt in the Low Countries* (Hambledon Press, 1990) A scholarly collection of interesting essays and articles, focusing particularly on the relationship between religious and political change in the Netherlands.

G.R. Elton: *Reformation Europe 1517-1559* (Fontana, 1990) First published in the early 1960s, Elton's Reformation Europe has stood the test of time better than his work on Tudor government. It is particularly helpful in putting the German Reformation into a wider political context.

M. Greengrass: *The French Reformation* (Historical Association Studies, Blackwell, 1987) A short, but immensely useful, survey of developments in France from the 1520s to the Wars of Religion.

A. Johnston: *The Protestant Reformation in Europe* (Longman Seminar Studies, 1991) A brief but comprehensive introduction to the Reformation, prepared with students of this level in mind.

H.A. Oberman: *Luther: Man between God and the Devil* (Fontana 1993) An usual and gripping biography of Luther which places him firmly in his medieval context. It is written by the leading contemporary historian of the Reformation.

M. Prestwich (ed): *International Calvinism, 1541 - 1715* (OUP, 1985) A collection of essays dealing with the impact of Calvinism on a European and, ultimately, global scale.

B.M.G. Reardon: *Religious Thought in the Reformation* (Longman, 1981) A particularly helpful introduction to the theology of the Reformation period.

R.W.Scribner: *The German Reformation* (Macmillan, 1986) Written by Britain's foremost historian of the German Reformation, this is a testing book for students at this level, adopting a thematic, rather than a chronological, approach.

INDEX